1 Longman Academic Writing Series

SECOND EDITION SENTENCES TO PARAGRAPHS

Linda Butler

This book is dedicated to a gifted teacher of the English language, and my teaching mentor, Jane Boggs Sloan.

Longman Academic Writing Series 1: Sentences to Paragraphs, Second Edition

Pearson, 221 River Street, Hoboken, NJ 07030

Staff Credits: The people who made up the *Longman Academic Writing Series 1* team, representing content creation, design, marketing, manufacturing, multimedia, project management, publishing, and rights management, are Pietro Alongi, Margaret Antonini, Eleanor Barnes, Gregory Bartz, Aerin Csigay, Gina DiLillo, Gina Eide, Warren Fischbach, Ann France, Shelley Gazes, Sarah Hand, Gosia Jaros-White, Stefan Machura, Amy McCormick, Bridget McLaughlin, Lise Minovitz, Linda Moser, Dana Pinter, Liza Pleva, Joan Poole, Katarzyna Starzynska-Kosciuszko, Joseph Vella, and Peter West.

Cover Images: BrAt82/Shutterstock (red quill pen), Evgeny Karandaev/Shutterstock (laptop).
Text Composition: MPS Limited
Cover Design: Page Designs International

Library of Congress Cataloging-in-Publication Data
Butler, Linda
 [Fundamentals of Academic Writing]
 Longman academic writing series. 1 : sentences to paragraphs / Linda Butler. — Second Edition.
    pages cm
 Previous title: Fundamentals of Academic Writing
 ISBN-13: 978-0-13-267938-1
 ISBN-10: 0-13-267938-8
 1. English language—Textbooks for foreign speakers. 2. English language—Rhetoric—
Problems, exercises, etc. 3. Academic writing—Problems, exercises, etc. 4. English language—
Grammar—Problems, exercises, etc. I. Title.
 PE1128.B854 2013
 428.2'4—dc23

                                                                2012045842

ISBN-13: 978-0-13-676995-8 (Student Book with App, Online Practice, and Digital Resources)
ISBN-10: 0-13-676995-0 (Student Book with App, Online Practice, and Digital Resources)

ISBN-13: 978-0-13-676987-3 (E-book with App, Online Practice, and Digital Resources)
ISBN-10: 0-13-676987-X (E-book with App, Online Practice, and Digital Resources)

Printed in the United States of America
8 2023

CONTENTS

To the Teacher x

Acknowledgments xi

Chapter Overview xiii

Chapter 1 **Introducing Yourself** 1

Introduction 2

    Looking at the Models 2

Looking at Vocabulary: Words for Names 3

Organization 4

    From Words to Sentences to Paragraphs 4

    Paragraph Format 5

Sentence Structure and Mechanics 5

    Sentence Structure 5

    Statements and Questions 6

    Sentence Mechanics 8

Grammar 10

    Verbs 10

    The Simple Present of the Verb *Be* 12

    Basic Sentence Patterns with the Verb *Be* 13

Applying Vocabulary: Using Words for Names 15

The Writing Process 16

    The Steps in the Writing Process 16

Writing Assignment: A Paragraph to Introduce Yourself 18

Self-Assessment 19

Expansion 20

    Your Journal 20

Chapter 2 **Everyday Routines** 22

Introduction 23
   Looking at the Models 23

Looking at Vocabulary: Word Partners.................25

Organization 26
   Formatting the Page 26

Grammar and Sentence Structure 30
   Nouns..30
   Subject Pronouns..33
   The Simple Present 35

Applying Vocabulary: Using Word Partners 37

The Writing Process 38
   Peer Review 38

Writing Assignment: A Paragraph about Your Morning Routine 40

Self-Assessment 42

Expansion 43
   On Your Own: A Paragraph about Your Sleep Habits...................43
   Your Journal 43

Chapter 3 **Every Picture Tells a Story**...................44

Introduction 45
   Looking at the Models 45

Looking at Vocabulary: *Go + -ing* Verbs.................47

Organization 48
   Topic Sentences..48

Sentence Structure 55
   Subjects of Sentences...................................55
   Writing Complete Sentences 56

Grammar 58
   Negative Verbs..58
   Adjectives 61

Applying Vocabulary: Using *Go + -ing* Verbs....................................63

Writing Assignment: A Paragraph about Someone in a Photo 64

Self-Assessment 67

Expansion 67

On Your Own: A Paragraph about Someone You Know Well 67

Your Journal 68

▧ Chapter 4 A Good Day....................................69

Introduction 70

Looking at the Models 70

Looking at Vocabulary: Phrasal Verbs....................................72

Organization 72

Time Order....................................72

Sentence Structure and Grammar 74

Simple Sentence Patterns, Part 1 74

Adverbs of Frequency....................................75

Using Prepositions to Show Time 79

Mechanics 81

Using Capital Letters 81

Capital Letters for Titles 82

Applying Vocabulary: Using Phrasal Verbs 83

Writing Assignment: A Paragraph about a Typical Day 84

Self-Assessment 86

Expansion 86

On Your Own: A Paragraph about a Favorite Holiday 86

Your Journal 87

▧ Chapter 5 Your Hometown 88

Introduction 89

Looking at the Models 89

Looking at Vocabulary: Words for Directions....................................91

Organization 92

    Supporting Sentences, Part 1 92

Grammar 94

    A, *An*, and *The* 94

    There Is and *There Are* 97

    Using Prepositions to Describe Location 99

Sentence Structure 100

    Prepositional Phrases in Sentences 100

Applying Vocabulary: Using Words for Directions 102

Writing Assignment: A Paragraph Describing Your Hometown.....................103

Self-Assessment 106

Expansion 106

    On Your Own: A Paragraph about a Favorite Place.............................106

    Your Journal 106

Chapter 6 On the Job 107

Introduction 108

    Looking at the Models...108

Looking at Vocabulary: Words for Jobs..110

Organization 111

    Supporting Sentences, Part 2 111

    Paragraph Unity..112

Grammar 114

    The Present Progressive..114

    Present Progressive vs. Simple Present 116

Sentence Structure 120

    Simple Sentence Patterns, Part 2...........................120

Applying Vocabulary: Using Words for Jobs.....................................123

Writing Assignment: A Paragraph about Someone at Work 124

Self-Assessment 127

Expansion 127

    Timed Writing: A Paragraph about Someone with a Good Job 127

    Your Journal 128

Chapter 7 Remembering an Important Event 129

Introduction 130

    Looking at the Models 130

Looking at Vocabulary: Adjectives + Prepositions 132

Organization 133

    Organizing Your Ideas 133

Sentence Structure and Mechanics 135

    Simple vs. Compound Sentences 135

Grammar 140

    The Simple Past 140

Applying Vocabulary: Using Adjectives + Prepositions 147

Writing Assignment: A Paragraph about a Memorable Event 148

Self-Assessment 150

Expansion 150

    Timed Writing: A Paragraph about a Weekend 150

    Your Journal 151

Chapter 8 Memories of a Trip 152

Introduction 153

    Looking at the Models 153

Looking at Vocabulary: Word Families 155

Organization 156

    Concluding Sentences 156

Grammar 159

    Past Time Expressions 159

Sentence Structure 163

    Sentences with Past Time Clauses 163

    Sentence Fragments 166

Applying Vocabulary: Using Word Families 167

Writing Assignment: A Paragraph about Your Memories of a Trip 168

Self-Assessment 170

Expansion 170

    Timed Writing: A Paragraph about a Childhood Experience 170

    Your Journal 171

Chapter 9 Looking Ahead 172

Introduction 173

    Looking at the Models 173

Looking at Vocabulary: Adverbs of Probability 175

Organization 176

    Listing Order 176

Grammar 178

    Expressing Future Time with *Be Going To* 178

    Expressing Future Time with *Will* 180

    Future Time Expressions 182

Sentence Structure 183

    Sentences with Future Time Clauses 183

    Run-On Sentences 186

Applying Vocabulary: Using Adverbs of Probability 188

Writing Assignment: A Paragraph about Your Future Plans 189

Self-Assessment 191

Expansion 191

    Timed Writing: A Paragraph about a Future Event 191

    Your Journal 192

Appendices

Appendix A More Ideas for Journal Writing 193

Appendix B Grammar Terms 194

Appendix C Grammar Charts 196

    1. Subject Pronouns; Object Pronouns; Possessive Adjectives;
       Possessive Pronouns 196

    2. Count and Noncount Nouns; Possessive Nouns 197

    3. The Verb *Be*—Present and Past 199

    4. The Simple Present 201

    5. The Present Progressive 203

    6. The Simple Past 205

    7. Irregular Verb Chart 208

    8. Expressing Future Time with *Be Going To* and *Will* 209

    9. Order of Adjectives 212

Appendix D Sentence Types (Simple, Compound, Complex) 212

Appendix E Mechanics (Rules for Capitalization, Punctuation) 214

Appendix F Correction Symbols and Practice 216

Index 219

Credits 222

TO THE TEACHER

Welcome to the new edition of Level 1 in the *Longman Academic Writing Series*, a five-level series that prepares learners of English for academic coursework. This book, formerly called *Fundamentals of Academic Writing*, is intended for beginning students in university, college, adult, or secondary school programs. It offers a carefully structured approach that helps students develop basic writing skills, understand writing as a process, and build a solid foundation for becoming independent writers.

Like the first edition, this book uses a clear, step-by-step approach as it introduces students to the requirements of academic writing in English. You will find a wealth of realistic models to guide student writers, along with clear explanations of sentence structure, paragraph organization, grammar, and mechanics. The explanations are followed by the extensive practice that learners need in order to assimilate the material and write with accuracy and confidence.

The text focuses on the elements of good sentences but within the context of simple descriptive and narrative paragraphs on student-centered topics. It effectively combines an introduction to basic paragraph structure with an emphasis on personal writing, the kind of writing that is most appropriate and motivating for learners at the beginning level. There are interactive tasks throughout the text—pair work, small-group activities, and full-class discussions—that engage students in the learning process and complement the solitary work that writers must do. There are also directions for keeping a journal so that students can write for fluency-building in addition to doing the more formal paragraph assignments. Finally, the extensive appendices and a thorough index make the text a valuable and easy-to-use reference tool.

What's New in This Edition

Instructors familiar with the first edition will find these new features:

- **Chapter objectives** provide clear goals for instruction;
- **Two new vocabulary sections**, *Looking at Vocabulary* and *Applying Vocabulary*, explain vocabulary from the writing models and support its use in the *Writing Assignment*;
- **Try It Out!** activities challenge students to be creative and apply the skills they have studied;
- **Writing Tips** contain strategies that experienced writers use;
- **Self-Assessments** ask students to evaluate their own progress;
- **Timed Writing** practice develops students' writing fluency;
- **Additional journal topics** appear in a new appendix.

The Online Teacher's Manual

The Teacher's Manual is available on the Pearson English Portal. It includes general teaching notes, chapter teaching notes, answer keys, reproducible writing assignment scoring rubrics, and reproducible chapter quizzes.

Acknowledgments

I would like to thank Ann Hogue and Alice Oshima, authors of the original Books 2, 3, and 4, for their work on the *Longman Academic Writing Series*. By creating these wonderful resources, they have served countless teachers and students of English over the years. I would also like to acknowledge the new members of the writing team for this edition: Jennifer Bixby, Jane Curtis, Lara Ravitch, and Alan Meyers.

I am grateful to the members of the Pearson ELT team for the expertise and dedication they have brought to this product, particularly Amy McCormick, Shelley Gazes, Lise Minovitz, and Eleanor Barnes. I also wish to thank my development editor Meg Brooks for her careful editing and wise counsel.

My thanks as well to the reviewers who contributed to our planning for this edition and those whose thoughtful comments and suggestions on the first edition also helped to shape this book:

Gena Bennett, Georgia State University, Georgia; **Vicki Blaho**, Santa Monica College, California; **Charlotte Calobrisi**, Northern Virginia Community College, Virginia; **Jackye Cumby**, Mercer University, Georgia; **Diana Davidson Del Toro**, Cuyamaca College, California; **Greg Davis**, Portland State University, Oregon; **Diane Harris**, Imperial Valley College, California; **Leisha Klentzeris**, Hodges University, Florida; **Shelagh Lariviere**, College of the North Atlantic, Qatar; **Linda Lieberman**, College of Marin, California; **Kathy Llanos**, Cypress College, California; **Gisele Medina**, Houston Community College, Texas; **Suzanne Medina**, California State University Long Beach, California; **Theresa Nahim**, Pace University, New York; **Tara Narcross**, Columbus State Community College, Ohio; **Mark Neville**, Alhosn University, Abu Dhabi, UAE; **Daria Ruzicka**; **Milagros Schwartz**, Community College of Baltimore County, Maryland; **Christine Tierney**, Houston Community College, Texas; **Lay Kuan Toh**, Westchester Community College, New York; **Stephen Whelan**, College of the North Atlantic, Doha Qatar.

I would also like to thank the following people for their feedback on an online survey: **Eric Ball**, Langara College, British Columbia, Canada; **Mongi Baratli**, Al Hosn University, Abu Dhabi, United Arab Emirates; **Jenny Blake**, Culture Works ESL, London, Canada; **Karen Blinder**, English Language Institute, University of Maryland, Maryland; **Bob Campbell**, Academic Bridge Program, Doha, Qatar; **Nancy Epperson,** Truman College, Illinois; **Kemal Erkol,** Onsekiz Mart University, Çanakkale, Turkey; **Russell Frank**,

Pasadena City College, California; **Jeanne Gross**, Cañada College, California; **Lisa Kovacs-Morgan**, English Language Institute, UC San Diego, California; **Mary Ann T. Manatlao**, Qatar Foundation, Academic Bridge Program, Doha, Qatar; **Ruth Moore**, University of Colorado at Boulder, Colorado; **Brett Reynolds**, Humber Institute of Technology and Advanced Learning, Ontario, Canada; **Lorraine C. Smith**, CUNY Queens College, New York.

In addition, I am grateful for the support and feedback provided by my ESL colleagues at Holyoke Community College, Massachusetts, in particular Rubaba Matin, Darcy Sweeney, Yulia Stone, and Lindsey Rothschild. I would also like to thank the following colleagues and friends for their help: Ismet Ozkilic and Valentyna Semyrog of Holyoke Community College; Mahmoud Arani of St. Michael's College, Vermont; Craig and Maggie Butler; and Hann Lam.

Finally, a special thank you and a round of applause to the students who shared samples of their writing with me, many of which have been adapted for this book: Julmarie Alvarado, Mary Benvenutty, Luz Blanco, Olga Bucalov, Wai Chan, Antonio Colon, Blasnelly Diodonet, Leslie Dones, Rose Feliciano Reyes, Lilybeth Garay, Alicia García, Juliana Gonzalez, Maryia Hancharonak, Zam Zam Hussein, Iryna Ivanova, Lisa Khomyak, Nataliya Kondratyuk, Mariya Korchevska, Nadia Kravchuk, Alice Lam, Iris Laviera, Keishla Martinez, Nelly Martinez, Oksana Morozova, Tam Kenny Nguyen, Mirjeta Nuhiu, Venhar Nuhiu, Moises Ortiz, Keisha Pacheco, Tatyana Pchelka, Viktor Rafalskiy, Genesis Ramo, Osmayra Rivera, Ina Ruskevich, Yelena Sokolova, Jason Son, Minja Son, Vera Stolyarova, Larisa Verenich, Penny Wu, and Yao Zheng.

—*Linda Butler*

Longman Academic Writing Series, Level 1, Sentences to Paragraphs offers a carefully structured approach to basic academic writing. It features instruction on paragraph organization, grammar, sentence structure, mechanics, and the writing process.

NEW! **Four-color design** makes the lessons even more engaging.

CHAPTER 1

INTRODUCING YOURSELF

OBJECTIVES

Writers need certain skills.

In this chapter, you will learn to:

- Put sentences into paragraph form
- Identify subjects and verbs in sentences
- Use capital letters and end punctuation in sentences
- Write sentences with the verb *be*
- Write, revise, and edit a paragraph to introduce yourself

It's nice to meet you!

1

INTRODUCTION

Before you write something, it helps to look at **models**. Models are examples. Model sentences will help you write your own sentences. Model paragraphs will help you write your own paragraphs. In this book, you will see many model paragraphs.

LOOKING AT THE MODELS

In the writing models, three students introduce themselves to their teachers and classmates.

Work with a partner. Read the models. Then check (✓) the information you find in each model.

🖉 **Writing Model 1**

> I would like to introduce myself. My name is Shaukat Matin. My nickname is Salim. I am from Pakistan. I speak Urdu. I am married. I live with my wife and our son. I want to study computers.

- ☑ name
- ☐ home country
- ☐ languages
- ☐ where he lives
- ☐ age
- ☐ family
- ☐ work
- ☐ classes at school
- ☐ free-time fun
- ☐ plans for the future

🖉 **Writing Model 2**

> I would like to introduce myself. My name is Marta Moreno. My full name is Marta Lucia Moreno Martinez. I am from Colombia. I am 19 years old. I live on campus. I like to go dancing. I want to travel.

- ☐ name
- ☐ home country
- ☐ languages
- ☐ where she lives
- ☐ age
- ☐ family
- ☐ work
- ☐ classes at school
- ☐ free-time fun
- ☐ plans for the future

2   CHAPTER 1

NEW! **Chapter objectives** provide clear goals for instruction.

Realistic writing models present the type of writing students will learn to produce in the end-of-chapter Writing Assignments.

NEW!

Looking at Vocabulary encourages students to notice useful words and phrases from the writing models that they can use in their writing assignments.

✐ Looking at Vocabulary: Phrasal Verbs

A **phrasal verb** has two parts: a verb (such as *go* or *get*) and a particle (such as *up, on,* or *out*). The meaning of a phrasal verb is often very different from the meaning of the verb alone.

He **gets** a lot of email.	*gets* = receives
He **gets up** early.	*gets up* = leaves his bed
His plane **gets in** at 1:00.	*gets in* = arrives

PRACTICE 1   Phrasal Verbs

Ⓐ Find these phrasal verbs in the writing models and underline them.

dress up	sleep in	eat out	go out	stay up

Ⓑ Match the phrasal verbs from the box with their meanings. Fill in the blanks.

1. _____ = put on nice clothes

2. _____ = not go to bed until late

3. _____ = leave home, often to do something for fun

4. _____ = have a meal in a restaurant instead of at home

5. _____ = stay in bed and sleep later than usual in the morning

ORGANIZATION

TIME ORDER

When you write a paragraph, you must think about organization. You must plan how to present information in a clear order. Writers need to organize information to make it easy for people to read. There are many ways to do this.

One way to organize information is to put it in **time order** (also called *chronological order*). This means writing about events in the order in which they happen. Start with the first or earliest event, and then tell what happens after that.

Time-order words help make information clear to the reader. They go at the beginning of sentences. A comma follows each one except *Then*. Do not put a comma after *Then*.

First,	Later,	Then	After that,	Next,	Finally,

72   CHAPTER 4

Clear instruction develops students' grasp of paragraph structure and organization.

PRACTICE 11   Capital Letters in Titles

Rewrite each title with the capital letters needed.

1. the adventures of Tom Sawyer

   The Adventures of Tom Sawyer

2. Harry Potter and the chamber of secrets

   _____

3. a tale of two cities

   _____

4. around the world in eighty days

   _____

5. the good, the bad, and the ugly

   _____

6. a journey to the center of the earth

   _____

Mark Twain, author of The Adventures of Tom Sawyer

✐ Applying Vocabulary: Using Phrasal Verbs

You saw some common phrasal verbs used in the writing models on pages 70 and 71:

dress up	get up	sleep in
eat out	go out	stay up

You may want to use some of those phrasal verbs when you do the Writing Assignment on page 84, writing about one day in a classmate's week.

PRACTICE 12   Using Phrasal Verbs

Ⓐ Complete the sentences with phrasal verbs from the box above.

1. When my alarm clock rings in the morning, it is time for me to

   _____ .

2. I do not set an alarm when I want to _____ .

3. I like to _____ with my friends for a movie or a concert.

(continued on next page)

A Good Day   **83**

NEW!

Applying Vocabulary shows students how to use new words and phrases in their writing.

Grammar and **Sentence Structure** sections in each chapter help students understand the building blocks of sentences. Clear charts with examples make the rules easy to see and remember.

GRAMMAR AND SENTENCE STRUCTURE

NOUNS

A **noun** is a word for a person, a place, a thing, or an idea. Look at the chart. The boldfaced words in the sentences are nouns.

NOUNS CAN BE:	EXAMPLES
1. Words for people	My **daughter** is at school. Do you know **David**?
2. Words for places	We usually eat in the **kitchen**. They are going to **San Diego**.
3. Words for things	I love **ice cream**. He drives a **Hyundai**.
4. Words for ideas	My **education** is important to me. Do you speak **French**?

Some nouns in the chart begin with capital letters: *David, San Diego, Hyundai,* and *French.* These words are **proper nouns**. A proper noun is the name of a specific person, place, thing, or idea. A proper noun always begins with a capital letter.

The other nouns in the sentences (*daughter, kitchen, ice cream, education*) are **common nouns**. A common noun does not need a capital letter.

PRACTICE 4 Identifying Types of Nouns

Work alone or with a partner. Write *person*, *place*, *thing*, or *idea* above each boldfaced noun in the paragraph. For some nouns, there may be more than one answer.

This is what I usually do in the **afternoon**. [*idea*]
I leave **school** and take the **bus** downtown with my [*place/thing*]
friends. I do not go home. My little **brothers** are
there, and the **television** is always on, so our
apartment is noisy. Instead, I go to the **library**. There
I can do my **homework**. On some **days**, I can get **help**
from a **tutor**. I like to look at **magazines**, too, like
Sports Illustrated. I usually spend two **hours** there.

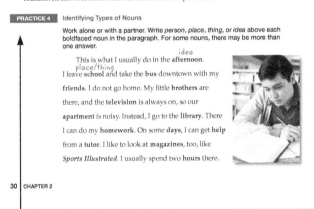

30 CHAPTER 2

Practice activities reinforce learning and lay the groundwork for the end-of-chapter Writing Assignment.

Editing skills are sharpened as students find and correct errors in sentences and paragraphs.

PRACTICE 10 Correcting Verb Errors

Find one verb error in each statement. Make corrections.

1. My best friend ~~is need~~ a new job. [*needs*]
2. My friend's name Massimiliano.
3. People calls him Max.
4. He work for a bank.
5. He is not like his job.
6. His job it's not the right job for him.
7. He is not want to stay at the bank.
8. He want to play his guitar all the time.
9. Max and his friends has a rock band.
10. They are good musicians, but they are not make any money.

TRY IT OUT! Work alone or with a partner. On a sheet of paper, write eight or more sentences about the Kim sisters. Use your imagination. Include both affirmative and negative verbs in your sentences.

Ronnie teaches math at a high school.
Allison does not have a job.
All the sisters have boyfriends.

The Kim sisters: Lizzie, Emily, Ronnie, and Allison

60 CHAPTER 3

NEW!

Try It Out! activities challenge students to apply what they have learned.

Step-by-step writing assignments make the writing process clear and easy to follow.

WRITING ASSIGNMENT

You are going to write a paragraph about a trip you took, like the writing models on pages 153 and 154. You will have a choice of prewriting activities.

Prewrite   **STEP 1: Prewrite to get ideas.**

a. Get ready to write by doing a prewriting activity. Choose one of these activities:
- Make notes about the trip in time order. (See page 133 for an example of notes in time order.)
- Freewrite about the trip for at least five minutes. (See page 134 for an explanation of freewriting and an example.)

Writing Tip

When you prepare to write a paragraph, think about your readers. What will they want to know about your topic? Working with a partner during the writing process helps you understand the needs of your readers.

b. Find a partner and take turns asking about each other's trips. Ask questions like these:
- Where did you go on your trip?
- When did you go?
- Who went with you?
- How long was your trip?
- What did you do on your trip?
- How did you feel about the trip?
- What do you remember most about your trip?

c. Look again at your notes or freewriting. Add information as needed. Include answers to the questions above. Underline the information that will be most important to describe your trip.

Write   **STEP 2: Write the first draft.**

Write your first draft. Begin your paragraph with a topic sentence. See the writing models on pages 153 and 154 for examples. Give details in your supporting sentences. Try to include both past time expressions and past time clauses. End your paragraph with a concluding sentence.

Writing Tips provide useful strategies to help students produce better writing.

Edit   **STEP 3: Revise and edit the draft.**

a. Read your paragraph again. It may help you to read it out loud. Make changes if needed.

b. Do peer review. Sit with a partner and exchange papers. Give each other feedback. Follow the steps on the Peer Review Worksheet.

PEER REVIEW WORKSHEET

Your partner's name: _____

Content

1. Read all of your partner's paragraph.
2. Underline any part of the paragraph you do not understand. Ask your partner to explain it.
3. Circle the topic sentence. If there is no topic sentence, write *TS?* on the paper.
4. Reread the supporting sentences. Ask questions if you want more information, or if it is not clear when the events happened.
5. Circle the concluding sentence. If there is no concluding sentence, write *CS?* on the paper.

Format and Language

6. Use this list to check your partner's paragraph. Check (✓) each item in the list as you finish.

☐ a subject in every sentence   ☐ the use of *before* and *after*
☐ a verb for every subject   ☐ the use of commas
☐ the use of past tense verbs

7. Put a question mark (?) if you are not sure about something.

Peer Review Worksheets help students give and receive constructive suggestions in a collaborative way.

c. Return your partner's paper. Can you say something nice about it?

d. Look at your own paper. If you do not agree with the feedback on it, ask another student or your teacher. Mark any changes you want to make.

Write   **STEP 4: Write a new draft.**

Writing Tip

Experienced writers know that good writing comes from re-writing. Do more than one draft and edit carefully.

a. Take a new sheet of paper and write a new draft.

b. Edit your new draft carefully. Then hand it in to your teacher.

NEW!

Self-Assessment encourages students to evaluate their progress.

SELF-ASSESSMENT

In this chapter, you learned to:
○ End a paragraph with a concluding sentence
○ Write past time expressions
○ Use *before* and *after* as prepositions
○ Write complex sentences with past time clauses
○ Identify and correct sentence fragments
○ Write, revise, and edit a paragraph about a trip

Which ones can you do well? Mark them ✓

Which ones do you need to practice more? Mark them ✗

EXPANSION

 TIMED WRITING

Students need to write quickly to succeed in academic writing. For example, sometimes students need to do a writing assignment in class or on a test, and they have only a short time to do it.

To practice writing quickly, you are going to write a paragraph in class. You will have 20 minutes. To complete the assignment in time, follow these steps.

1. Read the writing prompt below (or the prompt that your teacher gives you). Make sure that you understand the prompt. If you have questions, ask your teacher. (2 minutes)

2. Brainstorm to get ideas. On a piece of paper, make some notes. Then think about organizing your ideas. Mark up your notes with circles, arrows, and numbers to show the order of information in your paragraph. Write a topic sentence for your paragraph. (6 minutes)

3. Write your paragraph. Be sure to include a topic sentence, supporting sentences, and a concluding sentence. (10 minutes)

4. Check your paragraph. Correct any mistakes. (2 minutes)

5. Give your paper to your teacher.

   Prompt: Write a paragraph about an experience you remember from when you were a child.

170   CHAPTER 8

Expansion sections, such as timed writing, additional writing practice, and journal writing, encourage students to develop fluency.

EXPANSION

 ON YOUR OWN

Write a paragraph about your sleep habits. You can use "My Sleep Habits" as a title. You can begin your paragraph with one of these sentences:

   I am happy with my sleep habits.

   My sleep habits are not good.

1. Use these questions to help you take notes before you begin writing your first draft. Follow the steps of the writing process described on pages 40–42.
   • Do you get enough sleep, or are you often tired?
   • How many hours of sleep do you need?
   • What time do you usually go to bed?
   • What time do you usually get up?
   • Are weekday and weekend nights the same or different for you?

2. Write your first draft.

3. Ask a classmate to review your paragraph, or use the Peer Review Worksheet on page 41 to help you revise and edit.

4. Prepare a new draft, and give it to your teacher.

YOUR JOURNAL

Continue making entries in your journal. Write as much as you can. Write as often as you can.

Do not worry about writing perfect sentences. Your journal entries are not formal compositions. A journal entry is like a message to a friend.

You can think of your own topics for your journal entries. If you cannot think of a topic for a journal entry, try one of these ideas:
   • Write about a favorite food or drink. When and where do you have it? Do you make it, does someone make it for you, or do you buy it?
   • Draw a picture or put a photo in your journal. Then write about it.
   • Write about how you learn new words in English. Where do you find them? Do you write new words in a notebook? What kind of dictionary do you have?

For more ideas for journal entries, see Appendix A, page 193.

Everyday Routines **43**

NEW!

Timed Writing activities help prepare students to write well on tests.

CHAPTER 1

INTRODUCING YOURSELF

OBJECTIVES

Writers need certain skills.

In this chapter, you will learn to:

- Put sentences into paragraph form
- Identify subjects and verbs in sentences
- Use capital letters and end punctuation in sentences
- Write sentences with the verb *be*
- Write, revise, and edit a paragraph to introduce yourself

It's nice to meet you!

Before you write something, it helps to look at **models**. Models are examples. Model sentences will help you write your own sentences. Model paragraphs will help you write your own paragraphs. In this book, you will see many model paragraphs.

LOOKING AT THE MODELS

In the writing models, three students introduce themselves to their teachers and classmates.

Work with a partner. Read the models. Then check (✓) the information you find in each model.

🖉 Writing Model 1

> I would like to introduce myself. My name is Shaukat Matin. My nickname is Salim. I am from Pakistan. I speak Urdu. I am married. I live with my wife and our son. I want to study computers.

☑ name   ☐ family

☐ home country ☐ work

☐ languages   ☐ classes at school

☐ where he lives ☐ free-time fun

☐ age   ☐ plans for the future

🖉 Writing Model 2

> I would like to introduce myself. My name is Marta Moreno. My full name is Marta Lucía Moreno Martínez. I am from Colombia. I am 19 years old. I live on campus. I like to go dancing. I want to travel.

☐ name   ☐ family

☐ home country ☐ work

☐ languages   ☐ classes at school

☐ where she lives ☐ free-time fun

☐ age   ☐ plans for the future

✐ Writing Model 3

> *I would like to introduce myself. My name is Zhang Minxiong, but please call me Calvin. Zhang is my family name. Minxiong means smart and heroic. I am 21. I am taking classes in English and math. I live with my cousin and his family. I work part-time in his restaurant. I want to have my own business.*

☐ name   ☐ family
☐ home country   ☐ work
☐ languages   ☐ classes at school
☐ where he lives   ☐ free-time fun
☐ age   ☐ plans for
                       the future

✐ Looking at Vocabulary: Words for Names

Learning about words for names will help you introduce yourself. It will also help you learn other people's names. Look at the words for the name in the name tag.

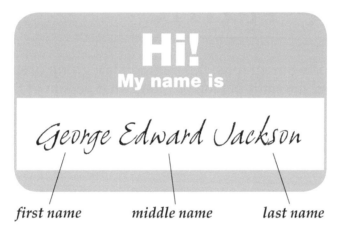

first name   middle name   last name

The words *last name* and *family name* have the same meaning.

PRACTICE 1 Names in Introductions

Ⓐ Look at the writing models. Find an example for each word in the list. Write the number of the model.

1. A first name: _____ Marta _____ in Writing Model __2__

2. A nickname: _____ in Writing Model _____

3. A full name: _____ in Writing Model _____

4. A family name: _____ in Writing Model _____

B Read the questions. Complete the answers.

1. What is your full name?

    My full name is _____.

2. What name do you want to use in this class?

    Please call me _____.

ORGANIZATION

FROM WORDS TO SENTENCES TO PARAGRAPHS

We use **words** to form **sentences**.

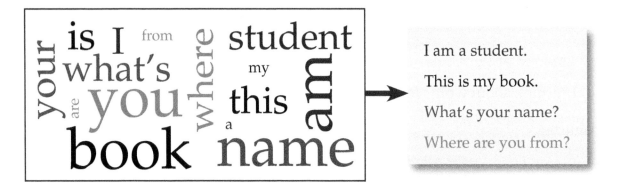

We use sentences to form **paragraphs**. A paragraph is a group of sentences. All the sentences are about the same person or thing. That person or thing is the **topic** of the paragraph.

The topic of the following paragraph is Yelena Politova. All the sentences in the paragraph are about Yelena.

> My classmate Yelena Politova is an interesting person. She is from Ukraine. She speaks Ukrainian and Russian. She lives with her family. She is married. She has one son and one daughter. She works part-time at an animal hospital. I hope to learn more about her.

PARAGRAPH FORMAT

Look at two things in the paragraph about Yelena.

- The first sentence is **indented**. There is a space before it. Remember to indent the first sentence when you write a paragraph.
- The second sentence follows the first sentence on the same line. It does not go on a new line.

INDENT   NEW SENTENCE, SAME LINE

⟶ My classmate Yelena Politova is an interesting person. She is from Ukraine. She speaks Ukrainian and Russian. She lives with her family. She is married. She has one son and one daughter. She works part-time at an animal hospital. I hope to learn more about her.

PRACTICE 2 Using Paragraph Format

These sentences are not in the form of a paragraph. Take a sheet of paper and copy the sentences in paragraph form.

> My classmate Jason Kim is an interesting person.
> He is from Seoul, South Korea. He speaks Korean.
> He is not married.
> He lives on campus. He has a roommate.
> He likes to play soccer and video games.

SENTENCE STRUCTURE AND MECHANICS

SENTENCE STRUCTURE

A **sentence** is a group of words that expresses a complete idea. A sentence has a **subject** and a **verb**.

SUBJECT VERB   SUBJECT VERB
Hiro plays the guitar.   He loves music.

The subject of a sentence can be a **noun**, like *Hiro*, *classroom*, or *students*, or it can be a **subject pronoun** (*I*, *you*, *we*, *he*, *she*, *it*, or *they*). The verb follows the subject. A verb often describes an action, like the word *play* or *eat*.

Work alone or with a partner. Circle the verb in each sentence. Write *V* above it. Then underline the subject of the verb. Write *S* above it.

                S   V

1. My class (has) 18 students.

2. We come from seven different countries.

3. The class starts every day at 9:00 A.M.

4. We meet in Building C, Room 301.

5. Our teacher is Mr. Robinson.

6. He is young and friendly.

7. He speaks slowly.

8. I understand him most of the time but not always.

9. I am a beginner.

10. In this class, all the students are beginners.

STATEMENTS AND QUESTIONS

There are different kinds of sentences. Some sentences are **statements**, and some sentences are **questions**.

Look at the example sentences in the chart.
- How are statements and questions the same?
- How are they different?

SENTENCES	
Statements	**Questions**
I am from Somalia.	Where are you from?
My name is Mumina.	What is your name?
I am a new student.	Are you a new student?
My first language is Somali.	Do you speak Spanish?

PRACTICE 4   **Word Order in Statements**

Work alone or with a partner. Put the words in order. Write statements.
Add periods.

1. is / My class / big _My class is big._

2. 24 classmates / have / I _____

3. from many countries / come / We _____

4. friendly / My classmates / are _____

5. Ms. Green / is / The teacher's name _____

6. We / in room 245 / meet _____

7. from / I / China / am _____

8. language / first / is / My / Chinese _____

PRACTICE 5   **Word Order in Questions**

A Work alone or with a partner. Put the words in order. Write questions. Add
question marks.

1. your name / What is _What is your name?_

2. How / your name / do you spell _____

3. from / are you / Where _____

4. What / your first language / is _____

5. live / do you / Where _____

6. are there in your family / people / How many _____

B What are the students in this picture saying? Write a question from Part A.
Write an answer.

SENTENCE MECHANICS

Sentences need **capital letters** and **punctuation**. A sentence begins with a capital letter and has a punctuation mark at the end.

RULES	EXAMPLES
1. Use a capital letter for the first word in a sentence.	T ~~t~~he class is in room 342.
2. Put a period (.) after a statement.	This sentence is a **statement**.
3. Put a question mark (?) after a question.	Do you have any **questions**?

PRACTICE 6   Capital Letters and End Punctuation

Add a capital letter to each sentence. Put a period after each statement. Put a question mark after each question.

A
1. ~~are~~ you married?

2. my friend speaks English

3. are you from China

4. he is from Mexico

5. do you drink coffee

6. our class starts at eight o'clock

7. where do you live

8. how do you spell your name

9. she works part time

10. we like to go dancing

PRACTICE 7   Editing for Errors with Capital Letters

Find four more missing capital letters. Make corrections.

M
~~my~~ name is Mayra. I am from the Dominican

Republic. my first language is Spanish. now

I live in Hartford. today is my first day in

this school. I want to learn English. it is very

important for my future.

Editing for Errors with Capital Letters and Periods

Correct the errors in this paragraph. Add five more capital letters and seven more periods.

> Kazumi is one of my classmates. ~~s~~**S**he is from Japan
>
> she speaks Japanese her parents live in Tokyo she has
>
> no brothers or sisters she is single Kazumi likes music
>
> and fashion her clothes are beautiful

TRY IT OUT! Complete the information about your class. Then take a sheet of paper and write your six sentences as a paragraph.

EXAMPLES

1. I am taking ___English 10___.
   (course name / number)
2. My class meets on ___Monday, Wednesday, and Friday___.
   (day or days)
3. It meets from ___9:30 A.M.___ to ___11:45 A.M.___.
   (start time)   (end time)

1. I am taking _____.
   (course name / number)

2. My class meets on _____.
   (day or days)

3. It meets from _____ to _____.
   (start time)   (end time)

4. We meet in _____.
   (building name / room number)

5. Our teacher's name is _____.
   (name)

6. The work is _____.
   (easy / hard / interesting)

VERBS

On page 5, you learned about sentences. A sentence needs a verb.

Some verbs are words for actions. This kind of verb describes movement or change. The verbs in these two sentences about Miki are action verbs. They tell what Miki does. You can see Miki in action.

Miki drives a convertible.

She sings.

Verbs do not always describe actions. The verbs in these two sentences about Miki do not describe any movement or change. They are non-action verbs. In the pictures, Miki is not doing anything.

Miki is a student.

She has friends at school.

Recognizing Verbs

Circle the verb in each sentence.

1. I have a cell phone.

2. I make calls to my friends every day.

3. My friends call me, too.

4. We talk a lot.

5. Sometimes my friends leave me a voicemail.

6. I listen to my messages.

7. Sometimes my friends send me text messages.

8. My phone has a camera.

9. I take a lot of pictures with it.

10. My phone is very important to me.

Building Sentences

Work alone or with a partner. Write six statements. Use words from the box. Use all six verbs.

Subjects	Verbs	
my friend my roommate he she	is goes has eats listens rides	a big family a new computer a student fish horses to movies to music

EXAMPLE

My roommate has a new computer.

1. _____

2. _____

3. _____

4. _____

5. _____

6. _____

THE SIMPLE PRESENT OF THE VERB *BE*

The words *am*, *are*, and *is* are verbs. They are the **simple present** forms of the verb *be*. The verb *be* is the verb that people use most often in English. *Be* is the **base form** of the verb.

The chart shows statements with *am*, *are*, and *is*. It shows **affirmative statements** and **negative statements**. To make a statement negative, use *not*.

Statements with the Verb *Be*

SINGULAR				PLURAL			
Subject	***Be***	***(Not)***		**Subject**	***Be***	***(Not)***	
I	am			We			
You	are			You			
He							
She		(not)	ready.	They	are	(not)	ready.
It	is						
Bill				Bill and Al			

See Appendix C3, page 199, for contractions with the verb be.

PRACTICE 11 **The Verb *Be* in Affirmative Statements**

Underline the subject of each statement. Write the correct form of the verb *be*.

1. This exercise _____*is*_____ easy.

2. I _____ a new student.

3. You _____ my partner.

4. We _____ on page 12.

5. My classmates _____ all here today.

6. The class _____ in Room C250.

7. My classes _____ all in one building.

8. You and I _____ in the same group.

9. The teacher _____ in the classroom.

10. Her first language _____ English.

Write negative statements. Use the correct form of the verb *be* + *not*.

1. You / late _You are not late._

2. The exercises / difficult _____

3. It / cold today _____

4. My friends / here _____

5. The teacher / in his office _____

6. You and Olga / in this group _____

7. I / hungry _____

8. We / on page 12 _____

BASIC SENTENCE PATTERNS WITH THE VERB *BE*

The verb *be* has many uses. Here are three ways to use *be* in sentences.

RULES	EXAMPLES
1. To identify a person or thing: Use *be* + a noun.	I am a new student. Mali is a country in Africa.
2. To tell where someone or something is: Use *be* + an expression of place.	Our room is on the third floor. I am from Lebanon.
3. To describe someone or something: Use *be* + an adjective or age.	Maria and Luis are married. I am 20 years old.

Sentence Patterns with the Verb *Be*

Work alone or with a partner. What follows the verb *be* in each of these statements? In each statement, underline the form of *be* and the words after it. Then circle *noun*, *place*, or *adjective or age*.

1. I <u>am 30 years old</u>.   *be* + **noun** / **place** / (**adjective or age**)

2. My nickname is Niko.   *be* + **noun** / **place** / **adjective or age**

3. I am not married.   *be* + **noun** / **place** / **adjective or age**

4. My family is not here.   *be* + **noun** / **place** / **adjective or age**

5. My parents are teachers.   *be* + **noun** / **place** / **adjective or age**

6. I am from a small town.   *be* + **noun** / **place** / **adjective or age**

7. My eyes are brown.   *be* + **noun** / **place** / **adjective or age**

8. My favorite sport is soccer.   *be* + **noun** / **place** / **adjective or age**

9. This work is easy.   *be* + **noun** / **place** / **adjective or age**

10. We are on page 14.   *be* + **noun** / **place** / **adjective or age**

Statements with the Verb *Be*

A Marco is writing about himself and his school. Complete Marco's statements with a subject from the box + *am*, *is*, or *are*.

I	My classmates	My name
My classes	My first language	My school

1. <u>My name is</u> Marco.

2. _____ from Panama.

3. _____ Spanish.

4. _____ a student.

5. _____ in Los Angeles.

6. _____ from many different places.

7. _____ interesting.

8. _____ 20 years old.

B Write true statements. Use the subjects from the box in Part A.
Use *am*, *are*, or *is*.

1. <u>My name is</u>

2. _____

3. _____

4. _____

5. _____

6. _____

7. _____

8. _____

Applying Vocabulary: Using Words for Names

You will write about your name when you write a paragraph to introduce yourself on page 18. Review the words for names on page 3.

PRACTICE 15   Writing Names

A Read the paragraph. Then complete the sentences. Write *first name*, *middle name*, *last name*, *nickname*, or *full name*.

> I would like to introduce myself. My name is
> Giancarlo Roberto Vitale. Please call me Johnny.
> I am from Rome, Italy.

1. His _____ is Giancarlo Roberto Vitale.

2. Giancarlo is his _____.

3. Roberto is his _____.

4. Vitale is his _____.

5. His _____ is Johnny.

B Review these sentences from the writing models on pages 2 and 3. Use them as models to write four sentences about yourself.

MODEL SENTENCES

My name is Shaukat Matin.

My nickname is Salim.

My name is Zhang Minxiong, but please call me Calvin.

Zhang is my family name.

Minxiong means smart and heroic.

YOUR SENTENCES

1. _____

2. _____

3. _____

4. _____

THE WRITING PROCESS

You are going to write a paragraph to introduce yourself. To write the paragraph, you will follow a **process**.

A process is a series of steps or actions. Many things we do in our everyday lives involve following a process. For example, we follow a process when we do laundry or when we follow a recipe to cook something.

Writers also follow a process. Following the steps in **the writing process** can help you write clear and correct paragraphs.

THE STEPS IN THE WRITING PROCESS

STEP 1: Prewrite to get ideas.

You begin the process by getting ideas for your paragraph. There are many ways to get ideas. You can look at models, make lists, or get ideas from talking with a partner. You will learn about other prewriting activities, too.

STEP 2: Write the first draft.

The first time that you write a paragraph, you produce your **first draft**. Your work is not finished! Writing the first draft is only one step in the process. Writers usually need to write more than one draft to produce good work.

STEP 3: Revise and edit the draft.

Revising and editing are important parts of the writing process.

- *Revise* means change. For example, you can revise a plan or revise your opinion about something. When you revise a paragraph, you add new information, take out sentences, or change the order of the ideas.
- *Edit* means check for mistakes and make corrections.

Sometimes you will do **peer review** before you revise and edit. Your peers are your classmates. When you do peer review, you work with a classmate as your partner. You read each other's paragraphs and talk about them.

STEP 4: Write a new draft.

Sometimes a writer's first draft needs no changes. This does not happen often! Most of the time, a writer needs to write two drafts—or more. Give your new draft to your teacher.

PRACTICE 16   Discussing the Writing Process

Look at the picture of the writing process. Talk about these questions with your class.

- What is happening in these pictures?
- Where does the writing process begin?
- What is the next step?
- What happens next?
- What happens after the teacher looks at a student's paragraph?

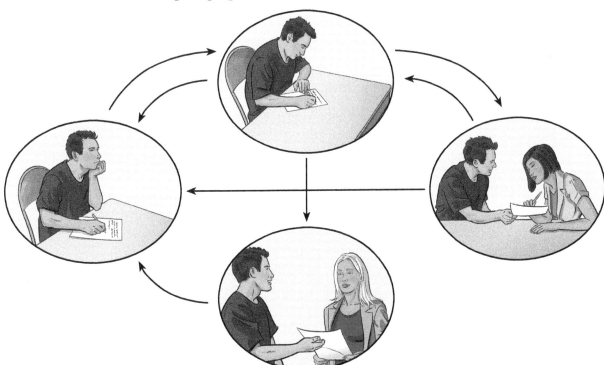

You are going to write a paragraph to introduce yourself. Follow the steps in the writing process.

Prewrite

STEP 1: Prewrite to get ideas.

a. Think about what information you want to give in your paragraph. Check (✓) five or more boxes in this list.

☑ my name   ☐ my family

☐ my home country   ☐ my classes at school

☐ the language(s) I speak   ☐ my job

☐ my age   ☐ what I like to do in my free time

☐ where I live   ☐ my plans for the future

☐ other information: _____

b. Look at the three writing models on pages 2 and 3. Underline any words or sentences you want to use in your paragraph.

EXAMPLE

> I would like to introduce myself. My
> name is Shaukat Matin. My nickname is
> Salim. I am from Pakistan. I speak
> Urdu. I am married. I live with my wife
> and our son. I want to study computers.

Write

STEP 2: Write the first draft.

a. Take a sheet of paper. Begin to write your paragraph. Indent the first sentence. Write:

> I would like to introduce myself.

b. Write sentences about yourself. Use your ideas from Step 1. Write your sentences in the form of a paragraph. This is your first draft.

Edit

STEP 3: Revise and edit the draft.

a. Work with a partner. Take turns reading your paragraphs out loud.
   - Is anything unclear? Tell your partner, "I don't understand."
   - Do you want more information? Say, "Tell me more about _____ ."

b. Do you need to make any of these changes to your paragraph?
   - Adding more information
   - Changing words
   - Adding capital letters or periods
   - Indenting

c. Mark any changes on your paper.

 Write

STEP 4: Write a new draft.

a. Take a new sheet of paper. Write your paragraph again.

b. When your new draft is ready, hand it in to your teacher.

SELF-ASSESSMENT

In this chapter, you learned to:

○ Put sentences into paragraph form

○ Identify subjects and verbs in sentences

○ Use capital letters and end punctuation in sentences

○ Write sentences with the verb *be*

○ Write, revise, and edit a paragraph to introduce yourself

Which ones can you do well? Mark them ✓

Which ones do you need to practice more? Mark them ⊘

YOUR JOURNAL

Keeping a **journal** can help you become a better writer. In a journal, you write about your life and your ideas. You can write in a notebook, or you can keep a journal online. An online journal is sometimes called a blog.

Each time you write in your journal, you make a **journal entry**. Your teacher will read your journal entries and write back to you about them. Your journal will be like a conversation between you and your teacher. In your journal, you can ask your teacher questions. Your teacher can ask you questions, too. Write the answers or talk to your teacher.

Your journal writing will be different from the other writing you do for this class. You will not need to correct any mistakes in your journal entries.

Frequently Asked Questions (FAQs) about Journals

1. What should I write about?

    You can write about things that happen in your life or things you are thinking about. You will also find ideas for journal entries in this book.

2. Who decides on the topic for a journal entry?

    Sometimes your teacher will give you a topic. Sometimes you can choose your own topic.

3. Who will read my journal?

    Your teacher will. You can share it with friends and classmates, too, if you want to.

4. How long should my journal entries be? How often should I write journal entries? How often will the teacher read them?

    Ask your teacher.

Look at this example of an entry in Murat's journal and the teacher's comments.

	April 26
	Soccer is my favorite sport. I played soccer at my high school. Now I
This is called	play with friends every day at 4:30 or 5:00 P.M. We play near the dining
"playing pick-up"	hall. Sometimes we have 6 or 7 players, sometimes 15 or 20. We don't
(when you play	have real games. We play for fun.
with anyone who	
comes).	*Great! I'm glad you have a chance to play your sport.*
	Do you ever watch soccer on TV?

1. Get a notebook to use for your journal. If you are writing your journal on a computer, follow your teacher's instructions. Remember to:
   - Put the date before each journal entry.
   - Leave margins on the left and right side of each notebook page.
   - Leave some space after each journal entry, too. Your teacher will need space in your journal to write back to you.

2. For your first journal entry, write about yourself. What do you want your teacher to know about you? What is important in your life?

For more ideas for journal entries, see Appendix A on page 193.

CHAPTER 2

EVERYDAY ROUTINES

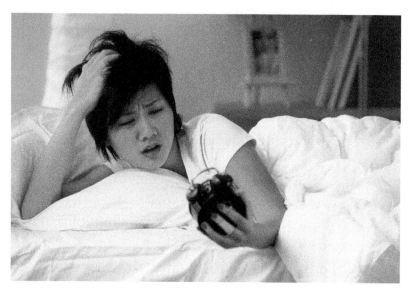

Time to get up

A morning run

A **routine** is your normal or usual way of doing things. If you usually do the same things every morning, you have a morning routine. In this chapter, you will write a paragraph about what you do to get ready for the day.

LOOKING AT THE MODELS

In the writing models, two students describe their morning routines.

Work with a partner or in a small group. Read the models. Then answer the questions.

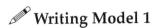 **Writing Model 1**

> ### My Morning Routine
> It is easy for me to get ready for the day. I wake up at
> 8:30 A.M., and I get up right away. I brush my teeth and wash
> my face. I get dressed and comb my hair. I check my phone
> for messages. Then I put it in my pocket. I put my books and my
> notebook in my backpack. I leave my room by 8:50 A.M. I walk to
> the University Language Center. My first class is from 9:00 to
> 10:20 A.M. After class, I am very hungry. I go to the dining hall
> and eat breakfast with my friends. That is my morning routine.

Questions about the Model

1. What is the topic of the paragraph? _____

2. Which word describes the writer's morning routine? Circle it: *(busy / easy)*

3. How much time does the writer need before class in the morning?

   _____

4. Where do you think the writer lives? _____

5. What words does the writer use to show time? Fill in the blanks.

   a. I wake up _____ 8:30 A.M.

   b. I leave my room _____ 8:50 A.M.

   c. My first class is _____ 9:00 _____ 10:20 A.M.

   d. _____ class, I am very hungry.

Getting Ready for the Day

I do many things to get ready for the day. My alarm goes off at 6:30 A.M., and I get up. First, I make coffee. Then I take a shower. I get dressed, fix my hair, and put on my makeup. At 7:15 A.M., I wake up my husband and my children. I help my children get dressed. Then we have breakfast. At 8:00 A.M., I walk my daughter to the school bus stop. After that, I drive my son to daycare. Finally, I go to school for my 9:00 A.M. class. That is my busy morning routine.

Questions about the Model

1. What is the topic of the paragraph? _____

2. What word describes the morning routine of this writer? Circle it: *(easy / busy)*

3. How much time does the writer need before class?

   _____

4. What **simple present** verbs does the writer use in these sentences? Fill in the blanks.

   a. My alarm goes off at 6:30 A.M., and I _____ .

   b. I _____ my children get dressed.

   c. At 8:00 A.M., I _____ my daughter to the school bus stop.

   d. After that, I _____ my son to daycare.

   e. Finally, I _____ to school for my 9:00 A.M. class.

5. What can you say about the morning routines of the Model 2 writer and the Model 1 writer? What is the same for both writers? What is different?

Looking at Vocabulary: Word Partners

Word partners are words that go together, like the verb *wash* and the noun *face* in *I wash my face*. Do not use the verb *clean* with *face*. Those words do not go together. Learning about word partners (also called *collocations*) will help you write better.

PRACTICE 1   Identifying Word Partners

A Circle the verb that goes with the boldfaced noun in each sentence. Find the sentences in the writing models on pages 23 and 24 to check your answers.

1. I *(clean / brush)* my **teeth** and wash my face.

2. I *(do / make)* many **things** to get ready for the day.

3. First, I *(do / make)* **coffee**.

4. Then I *(get / take)* a **shower**.

5. I get dressed, *(fix / make)* my **hair**, and put on my makeup.

6. Then we *(have / take)* **breakfast**.

B Complete the sentences with word partners. Use the verbs in the box. You can find all these verbs in the writing models.

check	comb	eat	leave	make	wash

1. First, I _____ my phone for messages.

2. Then I _____ my face with warm water and soap.

3. Next, I put on my clothes and _____ my hair.

4. After that, I _____ a pot of coffee.

5. At 7:30 A.M., I _____ breakfast.

6. I _____ my apartment at 8:05 A.M.

FORMATTING THE PAGE

You will write many paragraphs for this class. When you write a paragraph, you need to think about **format**—the way everything looks on the page.

Page Format for Handwritten Work

The paper

Use lined paper. Paper that is 8 1/2 by 11 inches is a good size.

The heading

The heading goes at the top of the page. It includes your name and the date. Your teacher may ask you to add other information, too.

The title

A title tells the topic of the paragraph. A title is not a sentence. It is just a few words or sometimes only one word. The title goes on the top line, in the middle.

Skipping lines

Do not write on the line below the title. Skip that line. Begin writing on the third line. The teacher may ask you to continue skipping lines. Skipping lines makes your paragraph easy to read. It also gives the teacher space to write in.

Margins

Leave spaces on the left and right sides of the page. These spaces are the margins.

Words at the end of a line

Sometimes a word is too long to fit at the end of a line. Do not divide the word into two parts. Move the whole word to the beginning of the next line.

Do *Not* Do This:	Do This:
I do not always take time for break-fast in the morning. Sometimes I skip it.	I do not always take time for breakfast in the morning. Sometimes I skip it.

The formatted page should look like this:

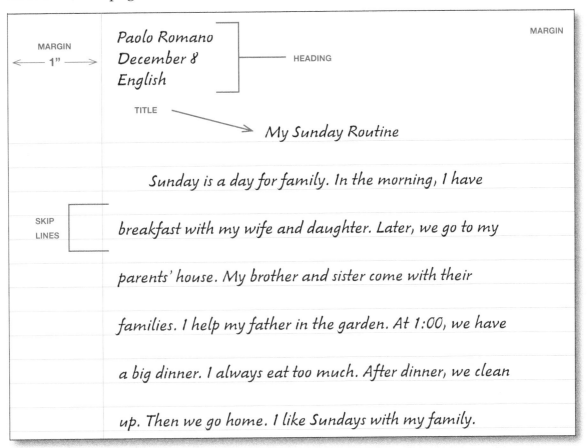

Identifying Errors in Format

A Work alone or with a partner. Look at Vu's paragraph. What problems do you see in the format? Mark them with circles or arrows.

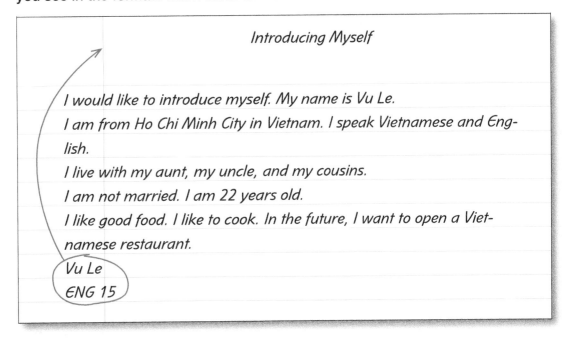

B Rewrite Vu's paragraph on a sheet of paper. Use the correct format.

Page Format for Work Done on a Computer

Margins

Set margins at the top and bottom of the page and on the left and right sides of the page. Make them about one inch (or 3 cm) wide. Most computer programs do this for you.

The heading

The heading goes at the top of the page. The heading includes your name and the date. The teacher may ask you to add other information, too.

The title

The title goes above the paragraph. Put it lower than the heading, centered on the page.

Line spacing

Double space your paragraph. The spaces between the lines make it easy to read. They give the teacher room to write.

Do *Not* Do This:	Do This:
These sentences are single-spaced. There is very little space between the lines. There is not enough space to write corrections.	These sentences are double-spaced. There is space between the lines for corrections.

Spaces in sentences

Leave only one space after each word. Do not leave a space before a period or other end punctuation.

Do *Not* Do This:	Do This:
This spacing is not correct .	This spacing is correct.

Saving your work

Remember to save your work. Ask your teacher how to name files.

Work alone or with a partner. Look at Deko's paper. Mark any problems you see in the format. Check the:

- Margins
- Heading
- Title
- Space between the lines
- Spaces in the sentences

My Computer

by Deko Hussein

My computer is helpful. I use it for school. I do homework on my computer. I also use my computer to write to my family and friends. Sometimes I use my computer for phone calls and video calls. I use my computer for the Internet, too. I use Facebook and watch videos online. I am very happy to have my computer.

NOUNS

A **noun** is a word for a person, a place, a thing, or an idea. Look at the chart. The boldfaced words in the sentences are nouns.

Nouns Can Be:	Examples
1. Words for people	My **daughter** is at school. Do you know **David**?
2. Words for places	We usually eat in the **kitchen**. They are going to **San Diego**.
3. Words for things	I love **ice cream**. He drives a **Hyundai**.
4. Words for ideas	My **education** is important to me. Do you speak **French**?

Some nouns in the chart begin with capital letters: *David, San Diego, Hyundai,* and *French.* These words are **proper nouns**. A proper noun is the name of a specific person, place, thing, or idea. A proper noun always begins with a capital letter.

The other nouns in the sentences (*daughter, kitchen, ice cream, education*) are **common nouns**. A common noun does not need a capital letter.

PRACTICE 4 Identifying Types of Nouns

Work alone or with a partner. Write *person*, *place*, *thing*, or *idea* above each boldfaced noun in the paragraph. For some nouns, there may be more than one answer.

                              idea

This is what I usually do in the **afternoon**.
   place/thing

I leave **school** and take the **bus** downtown with my

friends. I do not go home. My little **brothers** are

there, and the **television** is always on, so our

apartment is noisy. Instead, I go to the **library**. There

I can do my **homework**. On some **days**, I can get **help**

from a **tutor**. I like to look at **magazines**, too, like

Sports Illustrated. I usually spend two **hours** there.

Singular and Plural Nouns

Most nouns have **singular** and **plural** forms. *Singular* means "only one." *Plural* means "more than one." Plural nouns usually end in -*s*.

Some plural nouns are irregular. They do not follow the rules for plural nouns. They do not end in -*s*.

REGULAR NOUNS		IRREGULAR NOUNS	
Singular	**Plural**	**Singular**	**Plural**
1 hot dog	2 hot dogs	1 person	2 **people**
1 watch	2 wat**ches**	1 man	2 **men**
1 city	2 cit**ies**	1 woman	2 **women**
		1 child	2 **children**

See Appendix C2, page 197, for spelling rules, plural forms of regular nouns, and more irregular nouns.

PRACTICE 5   **Editing for Noun Errors**

Work alone or with a partner. Find 13 more errors. Make corrections.

I come from a big family. There are nine people~~s~~ in my immediate

family: my parent*s*, my three brothers, my three sister, and me. My

extended family is much bigger. It includes my four grandparent, 14

aunt, and 14 uncle. My aunt and uncle all have childrens, so I have

many cousin. Ten of my cousin are boy (or men), and 12 of them are girl

(or woman). When my family has a party, sometimes 50 or 60 relative

come to our house.

Count the people and things in the picture. Write 12 sentences with *There*. Use:

> *There is* + *one* + (singular noun).

> *There are* + (two or more) + (plural noun).

For help with spelling plural nouns, see Appendix C2 on page 197.

1. (man) _There is one man._

2. (child) _There are three children._

3. (woman) _____

4. (baby) _____

5. (person) _____

6. (family) _____

7. (table) _____

8. (banana) _____

9. (bowl) _____

10. (box) of cereal _____

11. (glass) of juice _____

12. (teapot) _____

SUBJECT PRONOUNS

A pronoun takes the place of a noun. A **subject pronoun** takes the place of a noun as the subject of a sentence. Look at this example:

He

Ahmed studies at home. ~~Ahmed~~ studies in his room.

THE SUBJECT PRONOUNS	
Singular	**Plural**
I	we
you	you
he	
she	they
it	

RULES	EXAMPLES
1. Use a noun or a subject pronoun, not both.	**My brother** has a new car. **He** has a new car. NOT: My brother ~~he~~ has a new car.
2. Use *it* to tell: • the time • the day • the date • the weather	It is nine o'clock. / It is 9:00. It is Wednesday. It is September 25. It snows in the mountains in winter.
3. Use *they* to refer to people or things.	**The children** are small. They are two years old. **The cars** are not new. They are two years old.
4. Use *I*, not *me*, as the subject of a sentence.	*My wife and I* ~~Me and my wife~~ get up early.

PRACTICE 6   Using Subject Pronouns

Write a subject pronoun in place of the crossed-out words.

1. My brother does not like to get up in the morning. ~~My brother~~ *He* likes to sleep.

2. My mother is an early riser. ~~My mother~~ gets up at 5:00 A.M.

3. My father likes mornings. ~~My father~~ is a morning person.

4. My roommate and I are not morning people. ~~My roommate and I~~ are night owls.

5. My alarm clock wakes me up in the morning. ~~My alarm clock~~ is loud.

6. My friends do not drink coffee in the morning. ~~My friends~~ prefer tea.

7. Our classes start early. ~~Our classes~~ start at 8:00 A.M.

8. What time is it? ~~The time~~ is 7:30.

9. How is the weather? ~~The weather~~ is warm and sunny today.

10. What is today's date? ~~Today's date~~ is February 2.

PRACTICE 7   Correcting Subject Pronoun Errors

Find one pronoun error in each statement. Make corrections.

1. My friends and *I* like to go out in the evening.

2. The evening it is my favorite time of day.

3. Is Saturday today.

4. He is the weekend.

5. Me and my friends want to see a movie.

6. Is a good idea.

7. Where are your friends? She are at the mall.

8. Is six o'clock now.

9. My friends and I we like scary movies.

10. How much are the tickets? Are $5 for students.

THE SIMPLE PRESENT

Use verbs in the **simple present** to describe routines and habits—actions that happen again and again. For example:

> I always **eat** lunch with friends.

> Our class **meets** at 7:00 P.M. on Tuesdays and Thursdays.

The form of a simple present verb depends on the subject of the verb.

SIMPLE PRESENT: AFFIRMATIVE STATEMENTS			
Singular Subject	**Verb**	**Plural Subject**	**Verb**
I You	sleep.	We You They	sleep.
He She It	sleeps.		

RULES	EXAMPLES
1. After *he, she, it*, or a singular noun subject, the verb ends in *-s, -es,* or *-ies*. These are **third person singular** subjects and verbs.	He **buys** things online. She **does** homework after school. My mother **worries** about me.
2. The verb *have* is **irregular**. It is not like other verbs.	I/You/We/They **have** juice. He/She/It **has** water.

See Appendix C4, page 203, for spelling rules for third person singular verbs.

PRACTICE 8   Using Simple Present Verbs

Complete each sentence. Write the correct form of the verb.

1. (have / has) I _____*have*_____ two roommates, Joe and Michael.

2. (do / does) My roommates and I _____ the same things every weekend.

3. (work / works) Joe _____ at a restaurant on Friday and Saturday nights.

(continued on next page)

4. (have / has) It _____ good pizza.

5. (eat / eats) I _____ there with friends every weekend.

6. (spend / spends) Michael _____ time outdoors on weekends.

7. (go / goes) He _____ for long rides on his bike.

8. (play / plays) He and his friends _____ soccer, too.

9. (have / has) Joe, Michael, and I _____ a good time on weekends.

10. (study / studies) On Sunday evening, we all _____ at the library.

| PRACTICE 9 | Spelling Third Person Singular Verbs |

Write the simple present verb. Use the third person singular form. For help with spelling, see the rules on page 203.

1. (fly) A pilot ___*flies*___ a plane.

2. (cook) Jason _____ for his family.

3. (fix) He _____ cars.

4. (wash) Who _____ the dishes?

5. (study) She _____ math.

6. (watch) Sarah _____ sports on TV.

7. (have) She _____ brown hair.

8. (rain) It _____ every day in some places.

9. (read) She _____ her email.

10. (go) Gina _____ to work by train.

| PRACTICE 10 | Correcting Verb Errors |

Find one verb error in each statement. Make corrections.

1. I ~~am~~ get up at 7:00 A.M.

2. First, I am take a shower.

3. A hot shower feel good in the morning.

4. We has a small TV in the kitchen.

5. Sometimes we watches the news on TV.

6. Pancakes my favorite breakfast.

7. We drinks coffee in the morning.

8. Coffee get me ready for the day.

✏ Applying Vocabulary: Using Word Partners

You will need to use word partners when you write about your morning routine on page 40. Review what you learned about word partners on page 25. Then study this list of verbs and nouns that go together.

Sometimes two verbs can go with a noun and both have the same meaning. For example, *I **have tea*** *in the morning* has the same meaning as *I **drink tea*** *in the morning.*

WORD PARTNERS	
Verb	**Noun**
drink/have	coffee, tea
make	a phone call
take	the bus, my car
wash/do	the dishes
watch	TV

PRACTICE 11   Using Verb + Noun Word Partners

Complete the sentences with verbs from the box. Choose the verb that goes with the boldfaced noun in the sentence.

~~check~~   do   fix   have   make   take

1. In the morning, I _____*check*_____ my **phone** for messages.

2. Next, I _____ a **shower**.

3. After that, I _____ **breakfast**.

4. Then I _____ the **dishes**.

5. Sometimes I _____ **phone calls**.

6. I _____ my **hair** before I go out.

Write five or more true statements about yourself. In each statement, use one verb and one noun from the boxes. Use word partners.

VERBS				
brush	do	fix	make	wash
comb	drink	have	take	watch

NOUNS				
breakfast	coffee	hair	tea	things
bus	face	shower	teeth	TV

EXAMPLE

Every morning, I make breakfast for my family.

_____

_____

_____

_____

_____

_____

THE WRITING PROCESS

Your writing assignment for this chapter will be a paragraph about your morning routine. To complete the assignment, you will follow the steps of the writing process.

Step 3 in that process is "Revise and edit the first draft." To help you revise and edit, you are going to do peer review.

PEER REVIEW

When you do peer review, you work with a partner and give each other **feedback**. You say what you think about your partner's paragraph, and your partner does the same for you.

When you look at your partner's paragraph, you need to think about these things:

- the content (the ideas and information)
- the words and sentences
- the page format

When you give feedback, it is important to be honest.

- When something in the paragraph is not clear, ask your partner, "What does this mean?"
- When the paragraph needs more information, say what you think is missing.
- When you see problems in grammar or spelling, tell your partner.

When you give feedback, it is also important to be kind. Remember that it is easy to hurt a writer's feelings. Always find something nice to say about your partner's work. For example, you can say:

"Your paragraph is interesting."

"I liked reading about _____."

"Nice work!"

"Thank you for showing me your paragraph."

PRACTICE 12 **Doing Peer Review**

Work with a partner. Henry and his partner did peer review. Look at the first draft. Answer the questions.

- What changes does Henry's partner think Henry should make?
- What do you think they talked about?
- Do you agree with the feedback?
- What other problems do you see with this draft?

Henry Liu
English 112-01
date   title   margin

It easy for me to get ready for the day. My alarm clock wake
          ^

                                    take
me up at 7:30. I get up and ~~have~~ a shower. Then I get

dressed.

                                                            sp?
I drive to school at 8:15. I go to the cafeteria. I very (hun-

your breakfast?
gry in the morning. I go to my class at 9:00. (that is my
              ^

morning routine.

Work with a partner. Look at Henry's second draft. Henry revised and edited his paragraph after peer review. What is different? What changes did Henry make and why?

Henry Liu
February 1
English 112-01

Getting Ready for the Day

It is easy for me to get ready for the day. My alarm clock wakes me up at 7:30 A.M. I get up and take a shower. Then I get dressed. I drive to school at 8:15 A.M. First, I go to the cafeteria. I am very hungry in the morning. I eat cereal, fruit, eggs, and toast. I drink juice and tea. I talk with my friends. Finally, I go to my class at 9:00 A.M. That is my morning routine.

WRITING ASSIGNMENT

You are going to write a paragraph about your morning routine. Follow the steps in the writing process.

 Prewrite

STEP 1: Prewrite to get ideas.

a. Take a sheet of paper. Make a list of the things you do in the morning to get ready for the day. Begin with the time you get up. Do not write complete sentences. Just take notes—write a few words.

> 7:00 A.M.—get up
> check phone
> shower, shave

b. Work with a partner. Ask your partner, "What do you do in the morning?" Take turns describing your morning routines. Try to use the words from the box.

first	then	next	after that	finally

Write

STEP 2: Write the first draft.

a. Choose a title for your paragraph. You can use one of these titles:

> Getting Ready for the Day
>
> My Morning Routine

b. Begin your paragraph with a general statement about your morning routine. Look at the writing models on pages 23 and 24 for examples.

c. Continue your paragraph, using your notes from Step 1.

 Edit

STEP 3: Revise and edit the draft.

a. Read your paragraph again. It may help you to read it out loud. Make changes if needed.

b. Do peer review. Sit with a partner and exchange papers. Give each other feedback. Follow the steps on the Peer Review Worksheet. Remember to be honest but kind.

PEER REVIEW WORKSHEET

Your partner's name: _____

Content

1. Read all of your partner's paragraph.

2. Underline any part of the paragraph you do not understand. Ask your partner to explain it.

3. Ask questions to get more information about your partner's morning routine.

Format and Language

4. Use this list to check your partner's paper. Mark any problems on the paper in pencil. Check (✓) each item in the list as you finish.

☐ the heading   ☐ spacing
☐ the title   ☐ a period after every statement
☐ indenting the first sentence

5. Put a question mark (?) if you are not sure about something.

See Henry Liu's first draft on page 39 for an example of how to mark a paper.

---

c. Return your partner's paper. Remember to say something nice about it.

d. Look at your own paper. If you do not agree with the feedback on it, ask another student or your teacher. Mark any changes you want to make.

Write

STEP 4: Write a new draft.

a. Take a new sheet of paper. Write your second draft.

b. Check your paragraph carefully. Then hand it in to your teacher.

Writing Tip

When you check for mistakes, read slowly. Sometimes using a ruler (or a sheet of paper) can help. Place it under the line you are checking. Move the ruler down as you read. Look at your paragraph word by word, one line at a time.

SELF-ASSESSMENT

In this chapter, you learned to:

○ Use correct page formats for paragraphs

○ Identify and use different types of nouns

○ Write and edit sentences with nouns and subject pronouns

○ Use simple present verbs in sentences

○ Give feedback on a partner's first draft

○ Write, revise, and edit a paragraph about your morning routine

Which ones can you do well? Mark them ✓

Which ones do you need to practice more? Mark them ⊘

ON YOUR OWN

Write a paragraph about your sleep habits. You can use "My Sleep Habits" as a title. You can begin your paragraph with one of these sentences:

I am happy with my sleep habits.

My sleep habits are not good.

1. Use these questions to help you take notes before you begin writing your first draft. Follow the steps of the writing process described on pages 40–42.
   - Do you get enough sleep, or are you often tired?
   - How many hours of sleep do you need?
   - What time do you usually go to bed?
   - What time do you usually get up?
   - Are weekday and weekend nights the same or different for you?

2. Write your first draft.

3. Ask a classmate to review your paragraph, or use the Peer Review Worksheet on page 41 to help you revise and edit.

4. Prepare a new draft, and give it to your teacher.

 YOUR JOURNAL

Continue making entries in your journal. Write as much as you can. Write as often as you can.

Do not worry about writing perfect sentences. Your journal entries are not formal compositions. A journal entry is like a message to a friend.

You can think of your own topics for your journal entries. If you cannot think of a topic for a journal entry, try one of these ideas:
   - Write about a favorite food or drink. When and where do you have it? Do you make it, does someone make it for you, or do you buy it?
   - Draw a picture or put a photo in your journal. Then write about it.
   - Write about how you learn new words in English. Where do you find them? Do you write new words in a notebook? What kind of dictionary do you have?

For more ideas for journal entries, see Appendix A, page 193.

CHAPTER 3

EVERY PICTURE TELLS A STORY

Who are the people in these photos? What are their stories?

When you look at a picture of someone new, you know some things about that person, but not everything. You can use your **imagination** to create a story about the person's life. Your imagination is your ability to form new ideas or pictures in your mind. In this chapter, you will use your imagination to write about a person in a photo.

LOOKING AT THE MODELS

Two students used their imaginations to write about the man in the photo. They have different ideas about him, so their paragraphs tell different stories about his life.

Work with a partner or in a small group. Read the models. Then answer the questions.

✎ **Writing Model 1**

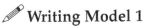

The Man in the Photo

The man in the photo is a hardworking man. His name is Ryan Murphy. He lives in Dallas, Texas. He is single. He lives with his two brothers. Ryan works in a factory. He works the second shift five days a week. He does not like this job. He wants a better job, so he goes to school. He is a part-time college student. He has classes three mornings a week. His classes are not easy. He works hard in school. In his free time, Ryan goes running and works out. On weekends, he plays basketball with friends. He leads a busy life.

Questions about the Model

1. What is the topic of the paragraph? _____

2. What is the writer's main idea about the topic? (Look back at the first sentence to find the answer.)

   _____

3. What information shows that Ryan is hardworking?

   _____

   _____

(continued on next page)

4. What verbs did the writer use in these sentences? Fill in the blanks.

    a. He _____ in Dallas, Texas.

    b. He _____ single.

    c. Ryan _____ in a factory.

    d. He _____ classes three mornings a week.

    e. His classes _____ easy.

5. Which sentences in items 4 a–e have the verb *be*?

Sentences _____ and _____ .

6. Which sentences have other simple present verbs?

Sentences _____ , _____ , and _____ .

✏ Writing Model 2

An Exciting Life

    The man in the photo has an exciting life. His name is Victor Torres. He lives in Hollywood. He is married. He and his wife do not have children. Victor works in the movie business and makes a lot of money. He drives a new Mercedes. He and his wife have a great house at the beach. It has a basketball court in the backyard. In his free time, Victor and his wife go dancing. They go to parties with famous people. They go shopping in Beverly Hills. Victor does not have any big worries. He is a lucky man.

Questions about the Model

1. What is the topic of the paragraph? _____

2. What is the writer's main idea about the topic? (Look back at the first sentence to find the answer.)

_____

3. What information shows that Victor has an exciting life?

_____

_____

4. What forms of the verb *have* did the writer use in these sentences? Fill in the blanks.

    a. The man in the photo _____ an exciting life.

    b. He and his wife _____ children.

    c. He and his wife _____ a great house at the beach.

    d. Victor _____ any big worries.

5. Which sentences in items 4 a–d have **negative** simple present verbs?

    Sentences _____ and _____.

✏ Looking at Vocabulary: *Go + -ing* Verbs

The verb *go* is often used with a verb ending in *-ing* to describe an activity.

    We **go swimming** in the summer.

    Do you ever **go bowling**?

PRACTICE 1   *Go + -ing* Verbs

A Look at the writing models. Find and circle these expressions: *goes running*, *go dancing*, and *go shopping*.

B Which of these activities do you do? Check (✓) your answers.

    ☐ go camping   ☐ go running

    ☐ go dancing   ☐ go shopping

    ☐ go fishing   ☐ go swimming

Do you ever go camping?

Writers need to make their paragraphs easy for readers to understand. One way to help the reader is to use a **topic sentence**.

TOPIC SENTENCES

A topic sentence comes at the beginning of a paragraph. The topic sentence gives the writer's main idea about the topic. A good topic sentence helps readers understand the paragraph.

The Parts of a Topic Sentence

A topic sentence has two parts:

- a **topic**—what the paragraph is about, and
- a **controlling idea**—what the writer is going to focus on in the paragraph.

```
        ─ TOPIC ─      ─ CONTROLLING IDEA ─
David Freeman is a good father.
```

This topic sentence tells the reader that the paragraph will be about David Freeman. It will be about David as a father. The paragraph will not have other information about David. For example, it will not tell the reader about his education, his friends, or his future plans.

Either the topic or the controlling idea can come first in a topic sentence. Compare these two topic sentences:

```
        ─ TOPIC ─     ──── CONTROLLING IDEA ────
Scuba diving requires careful preparation.
```

```
        ──── CONTROLLING IDEA ────     ──── TOPIC ────
You must prepare carefully before going scuba diving.
```

Sometimes the topic and the controlling idea are in two sentences. In this example, the topic is the twin sisters Emma and Alyssa. The controlling idea—that they have different interests—is in the second sentence.

Emma and Alyssa are twins. They look very much alike, but they have different interests. For example, Emma likes to . . .

Not all paragraphs begin with a topic sentence, but topic sentences are an important part of academic writing in English. You will need good topic sentences for paragraphs that you write as a student.

PRACTICE 2 Analyzing Topic Sentences

Find the topic sentence of each paragraph. Circle the topic and underline the controlling idea.

PARAGRAPH 1

The man in the photo has a terrible job. His name is Bob Walker, and he works for Bigg Computers. Every day, customers call him on the phone. They are unhappy about their computers. He does not like to listen to them. Sometimes they get angry, and they yell at Bob. Then he gets angry, too. He needs a new job.

PARAGRAPH 2

It is easy to make good chocolate chip cookies. Just buy a bag of chocolate chips at the supermarket and look for the recipe on the back. The recipe will list the other ingredients you need. At home, measure the ingredients and mix them to make the cookie dough. Put the dough into the refrigerator and wait for 24 hours. (That is the only hard part—waiting!) Follow the instructions to bake the cookies. The last step is the easiest part of all: eating the cookies warm from the oven.

PARAGRAPH 3

A betta makes a good pet for several reasons. First, it is a beautiful fish, especially in the sunlight. The light brings out its amazing color. Second, it is easy to take care of a betta. Just feed it every day, and give it clean water once a week. Finally, a betta is not expensive. You do not have to spend much money on the fish, its food, or its fishbowl. I tell all my friends to get a betta.

(continued on next page)

PARAGRAPH 4

My five-year-old nephew is a very funny little boy. I like to listen to him sing along with the radio. He often gets the words wrong. Sometimes he does it by mistake, and sometimes he does it on purpose, to make me laugh. I enjoy spending time with my funny little nephew.

PRACTICE 3 Choosing a Topic Sentence

Work alone or with a partner. Read each paragraph and the three sentences that follow it. Choose the best topic sentence for the paragraph and write it on the line.

PARAGRAPH 1

_____ He was the captain of two sports teams at our high school. He was our best wrestler and our best tennis player. He is also a good swimmer and a fast runner. He runs every day to stay in shape. Sometimes Kai and I play ping-pong together. Kai usually wins. He is good at ping-pong, too.

   a. Kai is a great friend.

   b. My friend Kai and I like sports.

   c. My friend Kai is good at sports.

PARAGRAPH 2

_____ For example, butterflies called Painted Ladies fly all the way from Europe to Africa. They also fly from Australia to New Zealand. Monarch butterflies fly from Canada to Mexico. That trip can be 3,000 miles long. It is amazing how far some butterflies can fly.

   a. Butterflies are beautiful.

   b. Some butterflies are great travelers.

   c. Butterflies live in many parts of the world.

A monarch butterfly

PARAGRAPH 3

_____ I like to have photos of family and friends to look at. I live far away from many of them now, and I miss them. The photos remind me of good times together. I also have many photos of my daughters growing up. It makes me happy to look at these photos and remember when my girls were babies. My daughters like to look at their old photos, too. The photos are fun for us to talk about.

    a. Photos are important to me.

    b. Everyone needs a good camera.

    c. Taking pictures can be quick and easy.

PARAGRAPH 4

_____ First, I admire her because she has many talents. She is a very good actor and singer. Second, she is also a movie producer, so I think she is smart. Finally, she seems like a good person. She visits schools to talk to teenagers about the value of education. She also talks about good health care for all women. I respect her ideas and her work. I hope she has a great career.

    a. America Ferrera is an unusual woman.

    b. I admire America Ferrera for several reasons.

    c. America Ferrera was in the TV series *Ugly Betty*.

TV and movie star America Ferrera

Topic Sentences and Titles

Each paragraph you write for a Writing Assignment in this book should have a title. The title and the topic sentence both help the reader understand what the paragraph will be about.

A title is usually not a complete sentence, and it does not do the job of a topic sentence. The topic sentence, not the title, has the topic and the controlling idea for the paragraph.

Writing Tip

It is a good idea to wait and write the title after you write your first draft of a paragraph. When you do that, the title does not affect your thinking about the topic sentence. Finish the first draft, check the topic sentence, and then add a title.

A topic sentence cannot refer back to the title, so sometimes the topic sentence must repeat words from the title. Do not begin a topic sentence with *He* or *She*, even when the person's name is in the title.

Do *Not* Do This:	Do This:
Gustavo's Favorite Day	Gustavo's Favorite Day
~~He~~ likes Saturdays because he can sleep in. He . . .	Saturday is Gustavo's favorite day of the week. He likes Saturdays because. . .

PRACTICE 4   Topic Sentences and Titles

Underline the topic sentence in each paragraph. Choose the best title for that paragraph and write it on the line.

PARAGRAPH 1

<u>Why I Like Classroom Discussions</u>

I enjoy classroom discussions for several reasons. For example, I like to hear my classmates talk. There are some interesting people in my class, and I like to hear their ideas and opinions. I also like to practice speaking English. Classroom discussions help me learn to speak better. They make time in class go by faster, too. These are just a few of the reasons why discussions make classes more interesting.

a. My English Class

b. Speaking English in Class

c. Why I Like Classroom Discussions

PARAGRAPH 2

_____

Everyone in my family loves music. We listen to music all the time. My parents like classical music and jazz. My sisters like popular music, and they love to sing karaoke. My brother likes rock music and plays guitar in a rock band. I like all these kinds of music at different times. People in my family sometimes argue about music, for example in the car, but we all agree on one thing. Life is better with music.

a. Music in My Life

b. A Family of Music Lovers

c. The Importance of Music

PARAGRAPH 3

_____

Bicycling is a smart form of transportation. A bicycle is inexpensive, so everyone can afford to own and ride one. Bicycles are quiet and clean, unlike cars or buses. Also, riding a bicycle is good exercise, and most people today need more exercise. More people should try bicycling to school or work. It is the smart way to get where you are going.

a. The Smart Way to Go

b. The Sport of Bicycling

c. Owning a Bicycle

PARAGRAPH 4

_____

My sister Anna is a very outgoing person. She loves to be with people, and she loves to talk. She has many friends, and she is on the phone with them all day long. She is happy to meet new people, too. She makes friends easily. She is never shy. She has a warm and friendly nature, and I am happy that she is my sister.

a. A Very Outgoing Person

b. My Sociable Sister

c. My Sister and I

Work alone or with a partner. Circle the topic and underline the controlling idea in each topic sentence. Then write two sentences you might find in that paragraph. Write a possible title for the paragraph.

1. **Topic Sentence:** (Cities) are exciting places to live.

    There are interesting things to do, like going to restaurants, movies, and clubs.

    You can meet many new people in cities.

    Possible Title: *The Benefits of City Living*

2. **Topic Sentence:** Cities have many problems.

    _____

    _____

    Possible Title: _____

3. **Topic Sentence:** Living alone is good in some ways.

    _____

    _____

    Possible Title: _____

4. **Topic Sentence:** Living alone is hard in some ways.

    _____

    _____

    Possible Title: _____

5. **Topic Sentence:** It is not easy to learn a new language.

    _____

    _____

    Possible Title: _____

6. **Topic Sentence:** There are many reasons to learn a new language.

    _____

    _____

    Possible Title: _____

SUBJECTS OF SENTENCES

In Chapter 1, you learned that a sentence has a subject and a verb. Here is more information about subjects.

Rules	Examples
1. A subject can be a noun or a subject pronoun.	NOUN SUBJECT PRONOUN Ryan likes sports. He watches sports on TV.
2. The subject comes before the verb in a statement.	S V On weekends, he plays basketball.
3. A verb can have more than one subject.	S S V Ryan and his friends play at the park.

PRACTICE 5   **Identifying Subjects and Verbs**

Work alone or with a partner. Find the subject and the verb in each sentence. Circle the subject and write _S_ above it. Underline the verb and write _V_ above it.

S   V
1 (My friend Mark Khajavi) is a talented photographer and a successful businessperson. 2 His photos are beautiful. 3 He takes pictures of people, places, and products. 4 People often ask him to take pictures at their weddings. 5 Companies hire him to take pictures of their products for advertisements. 6 Hotels and restaurants hire him to take pictures for their websites. 7 Most of the time, he works in Chicago. 8 Sometimes he travels to other parts of the country. 9 You can see examples of Mark's work on his website.

WRITING COMPLETE SENTENCES

These groups of words are not complete sentences. What is missing from each sentence?

INCORRECT: Is friendly.

INCORRECT: Has five people in her family.

Who is friendly? Who has five people in her family? The subjects of the sentences are missing. A sentence needs a subject. For example, you could write:

CORRECT: Bella is friendly.

CORRECT: She has five people in her family.

These groups of words are not complete sentences either. What is missing from each sentence?

INCORRECT: My brother in Los Angeles.

INCORRECT: Apples, bananas, and pears good.

There are no verbs in the sentences. A sentence needs a verb. For example, you could write:

CORRECT: My brother is in Los Angeles.

CORRECT: Apples, bananas, and pears taste good.

PRACTICE 6 Identifying Incomplete Sentences

Work alone or with a partner. Look at each sentence. Check (✓) *Complete* or *Incomplete*. Correct each incomplete sentence and identify the problem: Write *No subject* or *No verb*.

	COMPLETE	INCOMPLETE	WHAT'S THE PROBLEM?
1. a. The capital of China is Beijing.	☑	☐	_____
b. Beijing ^is a big city.	☐	☑	*No verb*
c. The city 5,000 years old.	☐	☐	_____
2. a. San Francisco has many attractions.	☐	☐	_____
b. Is cool in the summer.	☐	☐	_____
c. It has some interesting buildings.	☐	☐	_____
3. a. Many tourists travel to Mexico.	☐	☐	_____
b. Like Mexican food.	☐	☐	_____
c. Visit the beaches there.	☐	☐	_____

	COMPLETE	INCOMPLETE	WHAT'S THE PROBLEM?
4. a. The beaches of Thailand nice, too.	☐	☐	_____
b. Tourists like the beaches of Thailand.	☐	☐	_____
c. Many tourists photos.	☐	☐	_____
5. a. Sydney a city in Australia.	☐	☐	_____
b. It has a famous opera house.	☐	☐	_____
c. Many visitors to Sydney.	☐	☐	_____

Railay Beach, Thailand

PRACTICE 7   **Editing for Incomplete Sentences**

Find six more incomplete sentences in this paragraph. Make corrections.

1 My friend Yasmin is an interesting person. 2 She lives in Seattle, Washington. 3 *She is* ~~Is~~ young and single. 4 She 24 years old. 5 Works in a women's clothing store. 6 Is a nice place to buy clothes. 7 Yasmin likes her job. 8 Clothes very important to her. 9 Loves to shop. 10 She spends her money on new clothes and shoes. 11 She has a plan to open a clothing store. 12 She wants to have her own business. 13 It a good idea.

NEGATIVE VERBS

In Chapter 1, you learned about the verb *be* in negative statements. Review the information in the chart.

THE VERB *BE* IN NEGATIVE STATEMENTS			
Subject	**Be**	**Not**	
I	am		
You/We/They	are	not	ready.
He/She/It	is		

In Chapter 2, you learned about simple present verbs in affirmative statements. These verbs have two forms.

SIMPLE PRESENT VERBS IN AFFIRMATIVE STATEMENTS	
Subject	**Verb**
I/You/We/They	work.
He/She/It	works.

Simple present verbs in negative statements have three parts:

(1) *do* or *does*

(2) *not*

(3) the base form of the verb

SIMPLE PRESENT VERBS IN NEGATIVE STATEMENTS			
Subject	**Do/Does**	**Not**	**Base Form of the Verb**
I/You/We/They	do		
He/She/It	does	not	work.

See Appendix C4, page 201, for contractions.

Simple Present Verbs in Negative Statements

Underline the simple present verb in the first statement. Use the same verb to complete the second statement, but make it negative.

1. In soccer, the goalkeeper <u>catches</u> the ball with his or her hands. The other
   players ___do not catch___ the ball that way.

2. The goalkeeper wears gloves. The other players _____ gloves.

3. All the players on a team wear the team uniform except the goalkeeper.
   The goalkeeper _____ that uniform.

4. The goalkeeper stays near the goal. The other
   players _____ near the goal.

5. Some soccer players score goals. A goalkeeper
   _____ goals.

6. Most soccer players do a lot of running. The
   goalkeeper _____ so
   much running.

Affirmative and Negative Verbs

Ⓐ Complete the paragraph. Fill in each blank with the correct affirmative form
of the verb in parentheses.

My brother Raúl ___leads___ a busy life. He _____
                1. (lead)   **2. (have)**

a full-time job, and he _____ long hours. He
                            3. (work)

_____ good money, and he _____ spending
    4. (make)   **5. (enjoy)**

money. He _____ out on weekends with his friends. Raúl
                6. (go)

_____ eating in restaurants and going shopping. He
  7. (like)

_____ a nice car. On weekends, Raúl _____
  8. (have)   **9. (be)**

usually out having fun.

Ⓑ Rewrite the paragraph. Change *Raúl* to *Hector*. Make all the verbs negative.

    My brother Hector does not lead a busy life. He does not have
a full-time job, and . . .

Correcting Verb Errors

Find one verb error in each statement. Make corrections.

1. My best friend ~~is need~~ *needs* a new job.

2. My friend's name Massimiliano.

3. People calls him Max.

4. He work for a bank.

5. He is not like his job.

6. His job it's not the right job for him.

7. He is not want to stay at the bank.

8. He want to play his guitar all the time.

9. Max and his friends has a rock band.

10. They are good musicians, but they are not make any money.

TRY IT OUT! Work alone or with a partner. On a sheet of paper, write eight or more sentences about the Kim sisters. Use your imagination. Include both affirmative and negative verbs in your sentences.

Ronnie teaches math at a high school.

Allison does not have a job.

All the sisters have boyfriends.

The Kim sisters: Lizzie, Emily, Ronnie, and Allison

ADJECTIVES

The different types of words are called the **parts of speech**. Verbs and nouns are two of the parts of speech. **Adjectives** are another part of speech.

Adjectives are used to describe people, places, things, and ideas. The highlighted words in the example sentences are adjectives. Each of the adjectives describes a noun or a subject pronoun. The words described are boldfaced.

The **elevator** is full.	**He** is tall.	I like my new **phone**.

Look at the chart for rules on using adjectives in sentences.

RULES	EXAMPLES			
1. Use *be* + an adjective.		***Be***	**Adjective**	
	She I	is am not	intelligent. shy.	
2. Use an adjective + a noun.		**Adjective**	**Noun**	
	He is a	serious Close	person. friends	tell the truth.
3. You can use more than one adjective.	He is **young** and **handsome**. She has **short**, **dark**, **curly** hair.			
4. Do not add *-s* to adjectives.	Those girls are **good-looking**. NOT: Those girls are good-lookings.			

See Appendix C9, page 212, for information about the order of adjectives before a noun.

Adjectives and the Words They Describe

A Work alone or with a partner. Read the email. Decide if you think Jess likes the class or not. Then choose one of the two adjectives to fill in the blank and tell the story.

1. great / terrible
2. small / huge
3. comfortable / uncomfortable
4. interesting / boring
5. easy / hard
6. good / bad
7. interested in / tired of
8. best / worst

From: Jess49@xyz.co
To: Jo900@xyz.co

Hey, Jo, how's it going? I'm in my economics class, and it's

_____ . The class is _____ , and we're in a
      1.   **2.**

room with _____ seats. The professor is _____
           3.   **4.**

and _____ to understand, and she's always in a
     5.

_____ mood. My friend Chris is in this class, too. We're both
  6.

_____ economics. This is really my _____ class.
  7.   **8.**

Talk to you soon, Jess

B Look at the adjectives you wrote in Part A. Circle the noun or subject pronoun that each adjective describes.

I'm in my economics class, and (it)'s _____ *great* _____ .

On a sheet of paper, write six or more true statements about school. For example, you can describe your classes, your friends, or places at school. Use an adjective in each statement. Underline the adjective.

> I have <u>friendly</u> classmates.
>
> The cafeteria is <u>noisy</u>.

✎ Applying Vocabulary: Using *Go + -ing* Verbs

You saw the expressions *go running, go dancing,* and *go shopping* used in the writing models on pages 45 and 46. You also learned these expressions:

> *go camping*   *go fishing*   *go swimming*

You may want to use one of these expressions when you do the Writing Assignment on page 64, writing about a person you see in a photo.

PRACTICE 12   Using *Go + -ing* Verbs

Ⓐ Work in a small group. Ask the group about the activities in the list. When someone answers, "I do," ask that person "Where?" or "When?" or "Who do you go with?" Take notes.

Ask:		Names/Notes
Who goes	camping?	
	dancing?	
	fishing?	
	running?	
	shopping?	
	swimming?	

Ⓑ Take a sheet of paper. Use your notes to write eight or more true statements about the people in your group. Write affirmative and negative statements.

> Natasha does not go camping.
>
> Dao and her husband go fishing in the Gulf.
>
> Oscar goes running every day.

You are going to write a paragraph about a person in a photo, like the writing models on pages 45 and 46. You will need to use your imagination. Follow the steps in the writing process.

Prewrite   **STEP 1: Prewrite to get ideas.**

    a. Choose a person from one of these photos to write about. Imagine that you know the person well. On a sheet of paper, make a list of ideas about the life of the person in the photo. Do not write complete sentences. Just make notes.

Photo A

Photo B

Photo C

Photo D

b. Find a partner who has chosen a different photo. Ask your partner about the person in his or her photo. For example, ask:

- What is his/her name?
- Where is he/she from?
- Where does he/she live?
- How old is he/she?
- Does he/she have a family?
- Does he/she go to school?
- Does he/she have a job? What does he/she do?
- What does he/she like to do for fun?
- What do you think about his/her life?

c. Add to your notes or make changes, if needed.

 Write

STEP 2: Write the first draft.

a. Begin the paragraph with a topic sentence. The topic sentence should tell which person you are writing about and state the main idea about the person.

The woman in photo A has a/an _____ life.

The man in photo B is a/an _____ person.

b. Use an adjective in the topic sentence to describe the person or the person's life. In the paragraph, show your readers why that adjective is true for the person you are writing about.

c. Use your notes to complete the first draft. Add a title. See the writing models for examples of titles.

 **Edit**

STEP 3: Revise and edit the draft.

a. Read your paragraph again. It may help to read it out loud. Make changes if needed.

b. Do peer review. Sit with a partner and exchange papers. Give each other feedback. Follow the steps on the Peer Review Worksheet. Remember to be honest but kind.

PEER REVIEW WORKSHEET

Your partner's name: _____

Content

1. Read all of your partner's paragraph.

2. Underline any part of the paragraph you do not understand. Ask your partner to explain it.

3. Circle the topic sentence. If there is no topic sentence, write *TS?* on the paper.

4. Ask your partner questions if you need more information about the person in the photo.

Format and Language

5. Use this list to check your partner's paper. Mark any problems on the paper in pencil. Check (✓) each item in the list as you finish.

- ☐ the heading
- ☐ the title
- ☐ indenting the first sentence
- ☐ capital letters and periods
- ☐ a subject in every sentence
- ☐ a verb for every subject

6. Put a question mark (?) if you are not sure about something.

See Henry Liu's first draft on page 39 for an example of how to mark a paper.

---

c. Return your partner's paper. Remember to say something nice about it.

d. Look at your own paper. If you do not agree with the feedback on it, then ask another student or your teacher.

Write

STEP 4: Write a new draft.

a. On your first draft, mark any changes you want to make. Then take a new sheet of paper. Write a new draft.

b. Check your paragraph carefully. Then hand it in to your teacher.

SELF-ASSESSMENT

In this chapter, you learned to:

- ○ Use topic sentences in paragraphs
- ○ Identify noun and pronoun subjects of sentences
- ○ Identify and correct incomplete sentences
- ○ Use the negative forms of simple present verbs
- ○ Use adjectives to describe people, places, things, and ideas
- ○ Write, revise, and edit a paragraph about a person in a photo

Which ones can you do well? Mark them ✓

Which ones do you need to practice more? Mark them ⊗

EXPANSION

 ## ON YOUR OWN

Write a paragraph about a person you know well and like. Start by taking a sheet of paper and writing some notes about this person. Use the list of questions on page 65 for ideas. Think of some adjectives that describe this person. Decide on a topic sentence and write a first draft. Use the paragraph to help you.

> ### My Grandmother
>
> My grandmother is a helpful person. She helps our family, her friends, and people in the neighborhood. Everyone goes to her for advice. You can tell her about your problems. She listens and she does not tell your secrets to other people. She is patient and calm with my little cousins. She always talks to them in a quiet voice. We are happy to have our kind and helpful grandmother.

(continued on next page)

Ask a friend or a classmate to review your first draft. Ask your friend or classmate to use the Peer Review Worksheet on page 66. Then prepare a new draft and give it to your teacher.

 YOUR JOURNAL

Continue making entries in your journal. Remember to read your teacher's comments. Sometimes your teacher will write questions in your journal. Write the answers, or talk to your teacher about the questions.

If you cannot think of a topic for a journal entry, try one of these ideas:

- Who do you talk to on the phone? Name three people. When do you talk to them? What kinds of things do you usually talk about?

- Do you take photos or videos? Do you use a camera, your phone, or another device? Where do you keep your photos? How do you share them with friends?

- When do you usually do your homework? Where do you do it? Do you work alone, or do you work with other people? Do you listen to music while you work? Do you eat or drink while you work?

For more ideas for journal entries, see Appendix A on page 193.

CHAPTER 4

A GOOD DAY

OBJECTIVES

Writers need certain skills.

In this chapter, you will learn to:

- Use time order and time-order words in paragraphs

- Recognize two types of simple sentences

- Use adverbs of frequency in sentences

- Use prepositional phrases to show time

- Apply rules for using capital letters

- Write, revise, and edit a paragraph about a classmate's typical day

A day in the park

In this chapter, you will write about someone in your class, and someone will write about you. To get the information you need, you will **interview** each other. That means you will ask each other questions. Then you will write paragraphs about each other.

LOOKING AT THE MODELS

The writing models are about two students, Karl and Tomiko. Tomiko interviewed Karl and wrote about what he usually does on Fridays. Karl interviewed Tomiko and wrote about what she usually does on Saturdays.

Work with a partner or in a small group. Read the models. Then answer the questions.

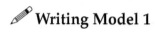 **Writing Model 1**

Karl's Fridays

Karl's Fridays are always busy days. He gets up early. Then he works from 6:00 A.M. to 2:30 P.M. After work, he gets his little boy from daycare. Sometimes they go shopping or play in the park. Then they go home. Karl's wife gets back from work at 5:30 P.M. They usually have dinner at home. In the evening, Karl puts his son to bed. Then he finally has time to relax. He and his wife sometimes watch a movie, but they do not stay up late. Karl is tired after his long day.

Questions about the Model

1. What is the topic sentence of the paragraph? Circle the topic and underline the controlling idea.

2. What information does the paragraph have about Karl's Fridays? Check (✓) your answers.

   ☐ what Karl does in the morning

   ☐ what he does in the afternoon

   ☐ what he does in the evening

   ☐ how he feels about Fridays

3. What simple present verbs did the writer use? Fill in the blanks.

    a. Then he _____ from 6:00 A.M. to 2:30 P.M.

    b. Karl's wife _____ back from work at 5:30 P.M.

    c. In the evening, Karl _____ his son to bed.

    d. Then he finally _____ time to relax.

✎ Writing Model 2

ꞁ ꞁ ◿◺ ꞁ ꞁ ꞁ ꞁ ꞁ ꞁ 1 ꞁ ꞁ ꞁ ꞁ ꞁ ꞁ ꞁ 2 ꞁ ꞁ ꞁ ꞁ ꞁ ꞁ ꞁ 3 ꞁ ꞁ ꞁ ꞁ ꞁ ꞁ ꞁ 4 ꞁ ꞁ ꞁ ꞁ ꞁ ꞁ ꞁ 5 ꞁ ꞁ ꞁ ꞁ ꞁ ꞁ ꞁ 6 △ ꞁ ꞁ

Tomiko's Favorite Day

Saturday is Tomiko's favorite day of the week. In the morning, she always sleeps in. Sometimes she does not get up until noon. Then she usually meets her friends in the dining hall. In the afternoon, they spend time outside or go shopping. It depends on the weather. On Saturday evenings, she likes to dress up and go out. She and her friends often eat out, see a movie, or go to a party. Tomiko loves Saturdays.

Questions about the Model

1. What is the topic sentence of the paragraph? Circle the topic and underline the controlling idea.

2. What information does the paragraph have about Tomiko's Saturdays? Check (✓) your answers.

    □ what Tomiko does in the morning

    □ what she does in the afternoon

    □ what she does in the evening

    □ how she feels about Saturdays

3. What does "It depends on the weather" mean? Circle *a* or *b*.

    a. The weather is not important to them.

    b. In good weather, they go outside; in bad weather, they go shopping.

4. What **adverbs of frequency** did the writer use? Fill in the blanks.

    a. In the morning, she _____ sleeps in.

    b. _____ she does not get up until noon.

    c. Then she _____ meets her friends in the dining hall.

    d. She and her friends _____ eat out, see a movie, or go to a party.

Looking at Vocabulary: Phrasal Verbs

A **phrasal verb** has two parts: a verb (such as *go* or *get*) and a particle (such as *up, on,* or *out*). The meaning of a phrasal verb is often very different from the meaning of the verb alone.

He **gets** a lot of email.	*gets* = receives
He **gets up** early.	*gets up* = leaves his bed
His plane **gets in** at 1:00.	*gets in* = arrives

PRACTICE 1   Phrasal Verbs

Ⓐ Find these phrasal verbs in the writing models and underline them.

dress up	sleep in	eat out	go out	stay up

Ⓑ Match the phrasal verbs from the box with their meanings. Fill in the blanks.

1. _____ = put on nice clothes

2. _____ = not go to bed until late

3. _____ = leave home, often to do something for fun

4. _____ = have a meal in a restaurant instead of at home

5. _____ = stay in bed and sleep later than usual in the morning

ORGANIZATION

TIME ORDER

When you write a paragraph, you must think about organization. You must plan how to present information in a clear order. Writers need to organize information to make it easy for people to read. There are many ways to do this.

One way to organize information is to put it in **time order** (also called *chronological order*). This means writing about events in the order in which they happen. Start with the first or earliest event, and then tell what happens after that.

Time-order words help make information clear to the reader. They go at the beginning of sentences. A comma follows each one except *Then*. Do not put a comma after *Then*.

First,	Later,	Then	After that,	Next,	Finally,

A Work alone or with a partner. Read the sentences. Then number them from *1* to *9* in time order.

_____ He turns the pancakes so they cook on both sides.

_____ Finally, he calls the children.

__1__ Martin likes to make pancakes for his children on Sunday mornings.

_____ Next, he gets out the eggs, milk, flour, and other ingredients.

_____ He mixes the ingredients in a large bowl.

_____ First, he puts the griddle on the stove to heat up.

_____ Then he pours spoonfuls of pancake batter onto the hot griddle.

__9__ Later, everyone will help clean up.

_____ They all sit down and enjoy a delicious breakfast.

Pancakes on the griddle

B Write the sentences from Part A as a paragraph.

Martin likes to make _____

_____

_____

_____

_____

_____

_____

_____

_____

_____

_____

Work alone or with a partner. Complete the paragraph with words from the box. For some sentences, there may be more than one possible choice.

After that	Finally	First	Later	Next	Then

Simone has a regular routine on Saturday mornings. She always gets up around 8:00 A.M. _____, she stretches and
1.
does some yoga. _____,
2.
she puts on her running shoes and goes for a run.

_____, she cools down by
3.
walking to a coffee shop. She orders coffee and

drinks it on her way home. At home, she takes a

shower and gets dressed. _____ she sits down and
4.
makes a list of things she needs to do that day. _____,
5.
she feels ready to start the day. _____, she will call a
6.
friend and make plans for the evening.

SENTENCE STRUCTURE AND GRAMMAR

SIMPLE SENTENCE PATTERNS, PART 1

There are several kinds of sentences in English. Understanding sentence patterns will help you write correct sentences.

First, there are **simple sentences**. A simple sentence has one subject-verb combination. Look at these two patterns for simple sentences:

1 subject + **1** verb	I like watermelon.
	Watermelon is my favorite fruit.
2 subjects + **1** verb	Alfredo and I like strawberries.
	Watermelon and strawberries are both delicious.

One or more subjects with the same verb means one subject-verb combination.

Simple Sentence Patterns

Circle the verbs and write *V* above them. Underline the subjects and write *S* above them.

1. In North America, S̲a̲t̲u̲r̲d̲a̲y̲ and S̲u̲n̲d̲a̲y̲ (are) weekend days.

2. In some other places, Friday and Saturday are the weekend days.

3. Saturday gets its name from the Roman god Saturn.

4. Monday means "moon day."

5. In the United States, elections are always on Tuesdays.

6. In Thailand, a color goes with each day of the week.

7. Green and orange are the colors for Wednesday and Thursday in Thailand.

8. In England, Monday, Tuesday, and Wednesday are lucky days for weddings.

ADVERBS OF FREQUENCY

Meanings

Adverbs of frequency tell how often something happens.

HOW OFTEN DO THEY EAT BREAKFAST?	SUN	M	TU	W	TH	F	SAT	
Alex **always** eats breakfast.	✓	✓	✓	✓	✓	✓	✓	100%
Uma **usually** eats breakfast.		✓	✓	✓	✓	✓	✓	
Olivia **often** eats breakfast.		✓		✓		✓	✓	
Saeed **sometimes** eats breakfast.	✓						✓	
Norberto **never** eats breakfast.								0%

Use *almost* with *always* or *never* to change the meaning to "nearly 100% of the time" or "nearly 0% of the time."

I **almost never** eat breakfast in a restaurant. I do that about once a year.

Placement in Affirmative Statements

The rules in the chart tell where to put an adverb of frequency in an affirmative statement.

RULES	EXAMPLES			
1. In most affirmative statements: Put the adverb before the verb.		**Adverb**	**Verb**	
	I	**usually**	arrive	on time.
	Tanya	**never**	comes	
2. In affirmative statements with *be*: Put the adverb after the verb *be*.		***Be***	**Adverb**	
	I	am	**often**	early.
	Jeremy	is	**sometimes**	

The adverb of frequency *sometimes* can also come at the beginning or end of an affirmative statement.

> **Sometimes** Jeremy is early.

> Jeremy is early **sometimes**.

| PRACTICE 5 | Adverbs of Frequency

Rewrite each affirmative statement. Add the adverb in parentheses.

1. (always) Valentine's Day is on February 14.

   Valentine's Day is always on February 14.

2. (usually) People think of Valentine's Day as a holiday for people in love.

   _____

3. (always) The dates of some holidays change, depending on the moon.

   _____

4. (never) Some people celebrate the new year on January 1.

   _____

5. (usually) Mother's Day is a popular holiday.

_____

6. (often) Schools are closed on holidays.

_____

7. (often) Workers have a holiday in their honor.

_____

8. (never) Some women work on International Women's Day.

_____

| PRACTICE 6 | Using *Sometimes* |

Rewrite each statement three times. Add *sometimes* in three different places.

1. My family has a special holiday meal.

_____

_____

_____

2. Stores are closed on holidays.

_____

_____

_____

Placement in Negative Statements

The rules in this chart tell where to put an adverb of frequency in a negative statement.

RULES	EXAMPLES		
1. Put the adverbs *always*, *usually*, and *often* after *not*.		**Not** **Adverb**	
	He does	**not** **always**	sleep well.
	They are	**not** **often**	late.
2. Put *sometimes* at the beginning of a negative statement.	**Sometimes** he does not call.		
3. Do not use *not* with *never*.	He is **never** ready on time.		
	NOT: He is~~n't~~ never ready on time.		

Rewrite each negative statement. Add the adverb in parentheses.

1. I am not at home on New Year's Eve. (never)

    I am never at home on New Year's Eve.

2. People in different countries do not have the same holidays. (always)

    People in different countries do not always have the same holidays.

3. Halloween is not an important holiday outside the United States. (usually)

    _____

4. Father's Day is not on a weekday in the United States. (never)

    _____

5. Some businesses do not close on holidays. (never)

    _____

6. For example, airports do not close on holidays. (often)

    _____

7. People do not celebrate every holiday in the same way. (usually)

    _____

8. In some countries, birthdays are not special days. (usually)

    _____

Happy New Year!

Look at the activities in the list. How often do you do these things? Take a sheet of paper, and write a true statement with an adverb of frequency about each activity.

watch the evening news on TV   write letters

drink milk   go shopping on weekends

get hungry in class   be in a bad mood

be tired in class

I almost never watch the evening news on TV.

USING PREPOSITIONS TO SHOW TIME

A **preposition**, such as *in, at, by,* or *with,* goes in front of a noun. The preposition and noun form a **prepositional phrase**. Prepositional phrases have many uses. For example, they can identify a place (*at home, in South America*) or a direction (*to school, up the stairs*).

Prepositional phrases can also be **time expressions**. Time expressions tell when something happens.

A time expression can go at the beginning or at the end of a sentence. Put a comma after a time expression at the beginning of a sentence.

PREPOSITION + NOUN
On **Saturdays**, I like to sleep late.

PREPOSITION + NOUN
I sometimes get up in **the afternoon**.

Here are five rules you need to know for using prepositions to show time.

RULES	EXAMPLES
1. Use *on* + a day or days.	Do we have class on **Friday**? They see each other on **weekends**.
2. Use *in* + a part of the day. Exception: Use *at* + *night.*	Call me in **the morning**. He gets home late at **night**.
3. Use *at* + a time.	He starts work at **8:30 A.M.** Lunch is at **noon**.
4. Use *from* + a starting point + *to* + the end point.	From **7:00** to **10:00 P.M.**, he studies. The course runs from **January** to **May**.
5. Use *for* + an amount of time.	They will be on vacation for **a week**.

See pages 99–100 and 160–162 for more information on prepositions.

Prepositions in Time Expressions

Underline six more time expressions with prepositions.

The Rock and Roll Hall of Fame in Cleveland, Ohio, welcomes music fans 363 days a year. The hall is closed only <u>on Thanksgiving and Christmas</u>. It is usually open from 10:00 A.M. to 5:30 P.M. On Wednesdays, it is also open in the evening. In the summer (from Memorial Day to Labor Day), it stays open late on Saturdays, too. There are exhibits, films, concerts, and a museum store. Each year, half a million people visit the Rock and Roll Hall of Fame. It is great fun for rock-and-roll fans.

Prepositions in Time Expressions

Complete the time expressions in the sentences. Use the prepositions *at*, *for*, *from*, *in*, *on*, and *to*.

1. Gary's rock-and-roll band always plays at a club _____ Saturdays.

2. The show starts _____ 9:00 _____ the evening.

3. The band usually plays _____ 9:00 _____ midnight.

4. In the middle of the show, they take a break _____ 10 minutes.

5. After the show, Gary stays at the club _____ a while.

6. He goes home _____ the early morning.

7. He usually goes to sleep _____ about 4:00 A.M.

8. He sleeps _____ 4:00 _____ noon.

USING CAPITAL LETTERS

Some words in English must begin with a capital letter. Here are five rules for capital letters that writers need to know.

RULES	EXAMPLES
1. Capitalize the subject pronoun *I*.	Rosa and I are in the same class.
2. Capitalize the first letter of a sentence.	His first name is David.
3. Capitalize people's names and titles.	My dentist's name is Dr. Parker.
4. Capitalize words for nationalities and languages.	**Nationalities** **Languages** Australian English Colombian Spanish Kuwaiti Arabic
5. Capitalize place names.	She lives in the Dominican Republic.

PRACTICE 10   **Correcting Capitalization Errors**

Find one or more capitalization errors in each sentence. Make corrections.

1. <u>T</u>the name of the song is "<u>M</u>michelle."

2. I have an appointment with doctor Patel.

3. Our teacher speaks spanish.

4. carlo is from new york.

5. my roommate drives a korean car.

6. susan's first language is english.

7. People speak tagalog in the philippines.

8. the man's nickname is red because of his red hair.

Work alone or with a partner. Look at the five rules for capitalization in the chart on page 81. Write two sample sentences for each rule.

Rule 4: *Maurício speaks Portuguese and English.*

1. Rule 1

_____

_____

2. Rule 2

_____

_____

3. Rule 3

_____

_____

4. Rule 4

_____

_____

5. Rule 5

_____

_____

CAPITAL LETTERS FOR TITLES

Follow these rules for using capital letters in the titles of your paragraphs.

RULES	EXAMPLES
1. Capitalize the first letter of the first word of a title.	My Life The Best Day of My Life
2. Capitalize every noun, verb, pronoun, adjective, and adverb in a title. Do not capitalize *a*, *an*, *the*, or prepositions.	A Day at the Races Take Me Out to the Ball Game
3. Do not put a period (.) after the title of a paragraph.	Getting Ready for the Day.
4. Do not put quotation marks (" ") around the title of a paragraph.	"Jae Yoon's Favorite Day"

Capital Letters in Titles

Rewrite each title with the capital letters needed.

1. the adventures of Tom Sawyer

   The Adventures of Tom Sawyer

2. Harry Potter and the chamber of secrets

   _____

3. a tale of two cities

   _____

4. around the world in eighty days

   _____

5. the good, the bad, and the ugly

   _____

6. a journey to the center of the earth

   _____

Mark Twain, author of The Adventures of Tom Sawyer

✏️ **Applying Vocabulary: Using Phrasal Verbs**

You saw some common phrasal verbs used in the writing models on pages 70 and 71:

dress up	**get up**	**sleep in**
eat out	**go out**	**stay up**

You may want to use some of those phrasal verbs when you do the Writing Assignment on page 84, writing about one day in a classmate's week.

PRACTICE 12 Using Phrasal Verbs

Ⓐ Complete the sentences with phrasal verbs from the box above.

1. When my alarm clock rings in the morning, it is time for me to

   _____ .

2. I do not set an alarm when I want to _____ .

3. I like to _____ with my friends for a movie or a concert.

(continued on next page)

4. I like to eat at home, but I like to _____ , too. I just like to eat!

5. I _____ when I go to a wedding or any formal event.

6. On New Year's Eve, I _____ late.

B Take a sheet of paper. Write six or more true sentences about what you do on Saturdays. In each sentence, use a phrasal verb from the box on page 83 and an adverb of frequency.

On Saturdays, I **never** sleep in.

I do not **usually** eat out on Saturdays.

WRITING ASSIGNMENT

You are going to interview a classmate about what he or she usually does on one day of the week. Your classmate will choose which day to tell you about. Then you will use the information to write a paragraph like the writing models on pages 70 and 71.

 Prewrite

STEP 1: Prewrite to get ideas.

a. Work with a partner. Ask your partner which day he or she wants to talk about. Then ask, "What do you usually do on that day?" Take notes in the chart. Do not write complete sentences.

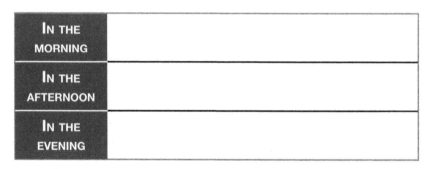

IN THE MORNING	
IN THE AFTERNOON	
IN THE EVENING	

b. What adjective best describes your partner's day? Talk with your partner about this question so that you can use this information to write a good topic sentence. You may want to use one of these adjectives in your topic sentence:

boring	exciting	interesting	tiring
busy	favorite	relaxing	

c. Write the topic sentence for your paragraph. Look at the writing models for ideas.

STEP 2: Write the first draft.

a. Begin your paragraph with your topic sentence from Step 1.

b. Continue writing your first draft, using your notes from Step 1.

c. Use time-order words, time expressions with prepositions, and adverbs of frequency, as needed.

d. Give your paragraph a title.

STEP 3: Revise and edit the draft.

a. Read your paragraph again. It may help you to read it out loud. Make changes if needed.

b. Do peer review. Sit with the person you wrote about and exchange papers. Give each other feedback. Follow the steps on the Peer Review Worksheet.

PEER REVIEW WORKSHEET

Your partner's name: _____

Content

1. Read all of your partner's paragraph.

2. Underline any part of the paragraph you do not understand. Ask your partner to explain it.

3. Tell your partner if any information is not correct.

4. Circle the topic sentence. If there is no topic sentence, write *TS?* on the paper.

Format and Language

5. Use this list to check your partner's paper. Mark any problems on the paper in pencil. Check (✓) each item in the list as you finish.

   ☐ the title   ☐ a subject in every sentence
   ☐ the use of words to show time   ☐ a verb for every subject

6. Put a question mark (?) if you are not sure about something.

   See Henry Liu's first draft on page 39 for an example of how to mark a paper.

---

c. Return your partner's paper. Can you say something nice about it?

d. Look at your paper. If you do not agree with a comment on it, then ask another student or your teacher.

 **Write**

STEP 4: Write a new draft.

a. On your first draft, mark any changes you want to make.

b. Take a new sheet of paper and write a new draft.

c. Edit your paragraph carefully. Then hand it in to your teacher.

Writing Tip

Before you give your new draft to the teacher, make sure that your paper is neat and formatted correctly. A careless paper makes a bad impression on the reader.

SELF-ASSESSMENT

In this chapter, you learned to:

○ Use time order and time-order words in paragraphs

○ Recognize two types of simple sentences

○ Use adverbs of frequency in sentences

○ Use prepositional phrases to show time

○ Apply rules for using capital letters

○ Write, revise, and edit a paragraph about a classmate's typical day

Which ones can you do well? Mark them ☑

Which ones do you need to practice more? Mark them ⊗

EXPANSION

 ## ON YOUR OWN

Write a paragraph about your favorite holiday. Begin by taking a sheet of paper and making notes about the things you usually do on this day. Organize your notes by time order. If you want, you can make a chart like the one on page 84.

Use your notes to write a paragraph. Begin your paragraph with a topic sentence, such as *Independence Day is always a lot of fun* or *New Year's Eve is my favorite holiday*. After you write your first draft, give your paragraph a title.

Ask a friend or a classmate to review your first draft. Use the Peer Review Worksheet on page 85. Prepare a new draft, and give it to your teacher.

Continue making entries in your journal. Do not worry about making mistakes. Your journal is a good place to experiment with new words.

If you cannot think of a topic for a journal entry, try one of these ideas:

- What is your favorite color? Do you have more than one favorite? What colors do you usually wear? Are there any colors you never wear?

- What are the seasons of the year where you live? Which season do you like most? What are some of your favorite activities during that season? Why?

- What languages do you know? Why are you learning English? Tell how you feel about learning English.

For more ideas for journal entries, see Appendix A on page 193.

CHAPTER 5

YOUR HOMETOWN

"Here is my hometown."

Your **hometown** is the place you think of as home. Maybe it is the place where you grew up. The word *town* usually means a small city, but a hometown can be of any size. In this chapter, you will write a paragraph about your hometown.

LOOKING AT THE MODELS

In the writing models, two students describe their hometowns.

Work with a partner or in a small group. Read the models. Then answer the questions.

✎ **Writing Model 1**

My Hometown

I am from Canóvanas, in the northeastern part of Puerto Rico, east of San Juan. My hometown is a small city with a big heart. There are about 30,000 people in Canóvanas. There are many good people in my hometown. When there is a problem, they are always ready to help. They are happy to take time out of their day to help a neighbor. My neighbors are like my family. That is the best thing about my hometown. I miss the friendly, helpful people of Canóvanas.

Questions about the Model

1. a. What is the topic of the paragraph?

_____

b. What is the writer's controlling idea about the topic?

_____

2. How many people live in Canóvanas?

There are about _____ people.

3. What sentences explain why the writer says that Canóvanas has "a big heart"? Copy one of them on the line.

_____

(continued on next page)

4. Where does the writer use the words *there* and *their*? Fill in the blanks.

    a. They are happy to take time out of _____ day to help a neighbor.

    b. _____ are many good people in my hometown.

    c. When _____ is a problem, they are always ready to help.

5. What is the difference between *their* and *there?* Circle the correct word to complete each rule.

    a. Use *(their / there)* + a noun to show possession.

    b. Use *(their / there)* + *is* or *are* to introduce new information.

✏️ Writing Model 2

ꞮꞮ Ⅹ ꞯ ꞯ ꞯ ꞯ ꞯ ꞯ 1 ꞯ ꞯ ꞯ ꞯ ꞯ ꞯ 2 ꞯ ꞯ ꞯ ꞯ ꞯ ꞯ 3 ꞯ ꞯ ꞯ ꞯ ꞯ ꞯ 4 ꞯ ꞯ ꞯ ꞯ ꞯ ꞯ 5 ꞯ ꞯ ꞯ ꞯ ꞯ ꞯ 6 △ ꞯ ꞯ

A Special City

Almaty, my hometown, is a special city. Almaty is in Kazakhstan. Kazakhstan is in the western part of Asia, south of Russia. My hometown is in the southeastern part of Kazakhstan, near China. The name Almaty means "the apple place." The first apples in the world grew in that area. My hometown was the capital of Kazakhstan for a few years, and it is still the cultural center of Kazakhstan. It has wonderful theaters and museums. Also, Almaty has the world's largest speed-skating rink. It is in the beautiful mountains outside the city. I do not live in Almaty anymore, but it is still a special place for me.

A speed skater inside a skating rink

Questions about the Model

1. a. What is the topic of the paragraph?

    _____

   b. What is the writer's controlling idea about the topic?

    _____

2. Where is Almaty?

    _____

3. Why does the writer think that Almaty is special? List three reasons.

_____

_____

_____

4. What prepositions does the writer use to show **location**? Fill in the blanks.

a. My hometown is _____ the southeastern part of

Kazakhstan, _____ China.

b. It is _____ the beautiful mountains _____
the city.

🖉 Looking at Vocabulary: Words for Directions

The words *north, south, east,* and *west* are used to describe locations and give directions. These words can be combined, as in *northwest*, for example. Add *-ern* to any of these direction words to form an adjective, such as *western* or *northeastern*.

PRACTICE 1   **Words for Directions**

Ⓐ Find five words for directions in the writing models. Circle the words.

Ⓑ Label the points on the compass with words from the box.

east	northeast	south	southwest
~~north~~	northwest	southeast	west

_____north_____

_____ _____

_____ _____

_____ _____

_____

In Chapter 3, you learned about introducing a paragraph with a topic sentence. A topic sentence needs **support**. It needs information that shows why the topic sentence is true.

SUPPORTING SENTENCES, PART 1

The sentences that follow a topic sentence are called **supporting sentences**. They support the topic sentence in the same way that the legs of a table support the tabletop.

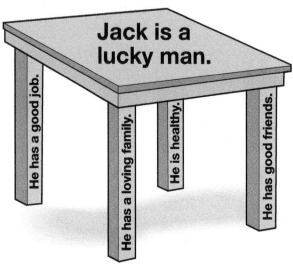

The supporting sentences show us why Jack is lucky.

Some paragraphs end with a **concluding sentence**. You will learn more about concluding sentences in Chapter 8.

Look at the three parts of this paragraph:

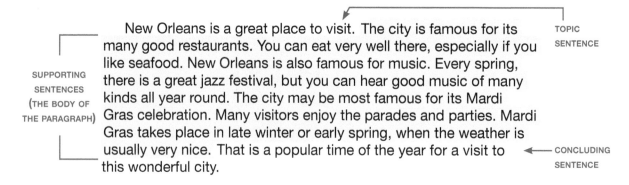

The paragraph has seven supporting sentences. They support the topic sentence "New Orleans is a great place to visit." They tell why the topic sentence is true.

Read the paragraphs and follow the directions.

Paragraph 1

The Weather in My Hometown

Hong Kong, my hometown, is a wonderful place for many reasons, but the weather is not one of them. Our best weather is in the fall, but we have a lot of air pollution. For this reason, we do not see clear blue skies very often. The winters are short but cool and damp. I feel cold all the time in the winter. In the spring, there is too much rain. In the summer, it is too hot and humid. Summer is also the season for typhoons. Typhoons are the worst part of Hong Kong's weather. I love my hometown, but I do not love the weather there.

a. Underline the topic sentence and the concluding sentence.

b. How many supporting sentences are there? _____

c. Complete this statement: The supporting sentences in this paragraph

tell why _____.

Paragraph 2

The Job of a Firefighter

Firefighters do a very important job. First of all, they put out fires in people's homes and workplaces. They also respond to emergency calls. The calls may be about dangerous situations, such as car accidents or heart attacks. Many firefighters are EMTs (Emergency Medical Technicians). They can help people with many kinds of medical emergencies. Every community needs firefighters.

a. Underline the topic sentence and the concluding sentence.

b. How many supporting sentences are there? _____

c. Complete this statement: The supporting sentences in this paragraph

tell why _____.

PARAGRAPH 3

How to Annoy a Roommate

It is easy to annoy a roommate. One way is to make a lot of noise. Do this especially when your roommate is sleeping or studying. Another way is to leave a mess on the floor. Drop your clothes and shoes everywhere. Finally, eat smelly food in the room. When you finish, put the dirty dishes on the floor, too. If you follow this advice, you will surely drive your roommate crazy.

  a. Underline the topic sentence and the concluding sentence.

  b. How many supporting sentences are there? _____

  c. Complete this statement: The supporting sentences in this paragraph show several ways to _____ .

GRAMMAR

A, AN, AND *THE*

The words *a*, *an*, and *the* are **articles**. Articles go with nouns.

Using *A* and *An*

RULES	EXAMPLES
1. Use *a* and *an* with singular nouns. • Use *a* before a consonant sound.	a **b**ridge, a **h**ouse, a **u**niversity
• Use *an* before a vowel sound. Think about the first sound—not the first letter—of the noun.	an **a**pple, an **h**our, an **u**mbrella
2. Do not use *a* or *an* with plural or noncount nouns.	My hometown has ~~a~~ parks. I need ~~an~~ information.
3. Use *a* or *an* when: • the noun is not specific	I need a pen. (Any pen—I do not care which pen.)
• the noun is first introduced	There is a huge park in my hometown.
4. One or more adjectives can come between an article and a noun.	**an** interesting **museum** **a** new, high-speed **train system**

See Appendix C2, pages 197–198, for information about singular, plural, and noncount nouns.

A Complete the definitions. Write *a* or *an*, or put a dash (—), meaning "no article."

1. __A__ capital is __a__ city where a state or a country has its main government offices.

2. __—__ museums are __—__ cultural attractions.

3. _____ hotel is _____ building where people pay to stay for a short time.

4. _____ inn is _____ small hotel.

5. _____ skyscrapers are _____ very tall buildings.

6. _____ theater is _____ place to see a movie or a play.

7. _____ amusement park is _____ place with rides, games, and other kinds of entertainment.

8. _____ roller coaster is _____ ride at _____ amusement park.

On a roller coaster

B Work alone or with a partner. Write sentences that describe the places and things in parentheses. Use the words from the box. Use *a* or *an* as needed. Add more information if you wish.

building	city	country	island	language

(Barcelona) *Barcelona is a city.* OR *Barcelona is a famous city on the coast of Spain.*

1. (Rio de Janeiro) _____

2. (Indonesia) _____

3. (the Taj Mahal) _____

4. (English) _____

5. (Aruba) _____

6. (the Eiffel Tower) _____

7. (Japanese) _____

8. (Montreal) _____

9. (the Maldives) _____

10. (Egypt) _____

Using *The*

RULES	EXAMPLES
1. The article *the* can be used with singular, plural, or noncount nouns.	Singular: the sun Plural: the stars Noncount: the weather
2. Use *the* when the noun means a specific person, place, thing, or idea.	Specific: London is the **capital of England**. Not specific: London is a **city**.
3. Use *the* when you repeat a noun already introduced.	There is a **stadium** in my hometown. I watch soccer matches at the **stadium**.

PRACTICE 4 Using *A*, *An*, or *The*

Complete the sentences. Write *a*, *an*, or *the*.

1. In my hometown, there is _____ small college and
   a.
   _____ large university. _____ college has about
   b.   c.
   1,200 students. _____ university has about 35,000.
                   d.

2. _____ aquarium is _____ building where people
   a.   b.
   can see fish and other sea animals. My hometown has _____
                                                       c.
   new aquarium. _____ aquarium in my hometown is
                 d.
   _____ interesting place to visit.
   e.

3. They are building _____ airport near my city. There is already
                     a.
   _____ airport there, but it is small. _____ new
   b.   c.
   airport will be big.

4. I am from Jakarta. It is _____ capital of Indonesia. It is on
                           a.
   _____ northwest coast of Java. Java is _____ island.
   b.   c.

THERE IS AND THERE ARE

Sentences with *there is* and *there are* often introduce new information.

NEW INFORMATION

There is **no school on Friday!**

In addition, sentences with *there is* and *there are* often:

- tell the time of something

    There is a train **at 7:30 A.M.**

- tell where someone or something is

    There are good restaurants **in my hometown**.

STATEMENTS WITH *THERE IS* AND *THERE ARE*							
There	**Is**	**Singular Noun/ Noncount Noun**		**There**	**Are**	**Plural Noun**	
There	is	a lake	in my hometown.	There	are	four people	in my family.
		music	on the radio.			many things	to see and do.

See Appendix C2, pages 197–198, for information about singular, plural, and noncount nouns.

RULES	EXAMPLES
1. Use *there is/are* + *no* + noun to form a negative statement.	There is **no** stadium in my city. There are **no** tall buildings in my hometown. There is **no** snow in the winter.
2. Do not confuse *there are* with *they are*. • Use *there are* to introduce new information. • Use *they* instead of repeating a noun.	NEW INFORMATION There are two rivers in my city. *They* ~~The two rivers~~ are the Danube and the Sava.
3. Do not confuse *there* with *their*. • Use *there* + *is* or *are*. • Use *their* + a noun. *Their* shows possession.	There **are** two girls in the group. Their **names** are Isabel and Pilar.

There Is or *There Are*

Complete the sentences. Write *there is* or *there are*.

_____ many shopping malls in North America, but
    1.
the West Edmonton Mall in Canada is the biggest. _____
                                                        2.
more than 800 stores in the mall. A visitor to the mall can shop for

days. _____ many other things to do, too. For example,
          3.

_____ a skating rink, _____ many amusement
        4.   5.
park rides, and _____ a theater with eight movie
                        6.
screens. _____ 20 restaurants for hungry shoppers, and
              7.
_____ even a hotel. _____ something for
        8.   9.
everyone at the West Edmonton Mall.

PRACTICE 6   Correcting Errors with *There*, *Their*, and *They*

Find nine more errors with *there*, *their*, and *they*. Make corrections.

  There
1. ~~They~~ are two students from Korea in my class. There names are Jun Seong

   and Min Sup. They usually sit in the first row, but their absent today.

2. The teachers often meet on Wednesdays. There meetings take place in the

   conference room. Their is a large round table in the room. There usually

   have there lunch during the meetings.

3. They are about 100 students in this program. There are from several

   different countries. Their learning English.

TRY IT OUT!   Take a sheet of paper. Write your answers to the questions. Use *There is* or
               There are.

  There are three floors in my building.

1. How many floors are there in the building where you live?

2. How many pictures are there on the walls of your room?

3. How many people are there in your family?

4. How many movie theaters are there in your hometown?

5. How many doors are there to your classroom?

6. How many students are there in your class?

USING PREPOSITIONS TO DESCRIBE LOCATION

In Chapter 4, you learned about using prepositions in time expressions. Prepositions are also used to describe location—where someone or something is. These prepositions include *between, next to, in front of, in back of, near, in, on,* and *at.*

Costa Rica is **next to** Nicaragua.

Costa Rica is **between** Nicaragua and Panama.

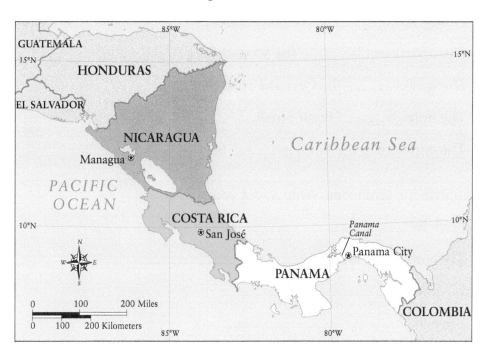

Study the rules for using *in, on,* and *at* to describe location.

RULES	EXAMPLES
1. Use *in* + a continent, country, state, province, or city.	Canada is in **North America**. There are ten provinces in **Canada**. The beautiful city of Vancouver is in **British Columbia**. My cousins live in **Vancouver**.
2. Use *on* + a street (without a specific address) or a floor of a building.	Their office building is on **King Street**. We are meeting on **the tenth floor**.
3. Use *at* + a specific address or building.	The Kelleys live at **132 Maple Street**. He works at **the hospital**.

PRACTICE 7　　*In*, *On*, and *At* for Location

Ⓐ Complete the sentences with *in*, *on*, or *at*.

1. Nina lives _____ California.

2. California is _____ the United States.

3. She lives _____ Water Street _____ San Francisco.

4. Her building is _____ 94 Water Street.

5. Her apartment is _____ the second floor.

6. She works _____ the Orchard Hotel.

7. The hotel is _____ Bush Street.

8. The entrance to the hotel is _____ 665 Bush Street.

Ⓑ Complete the sentences. Write about yourself.

1. I live **in** _____ .

2. My hometown is **in** _____ .

3. I live **on** _____ .

4. I live **at** _____ .

SENTENCE STRUCTURE

PREPOSITIONAL PHRASES IN SENTENCES

In Chapter 4, you learned that a preposition and a noun form a prepositional phrase. A writer can put a prepositional phrase in several places in a sentence.

RULES	EXAMPLES
1. A prepositional phrase can come: • after the verb *be* • after other verbs • after a noun	Dakar **is** in Senegal. Miguel **comes** from Mexico City. The **weather** in India is usually hot.
2. A prepositional phrase can also come at the beginning or end of a sentence. Put a comma after a prepositional phrase at the beginning of a sentence.	There are beautiful forests in my country. In my country, there are beautiful forests.

Prepositional Phrases in Sentences

Underline the prepositional phrases in the examples on the right. Then match the patterns and examples. Write the letters.

PATTERNS

___b___ 1. *be* + prepositional phrase
_____ 2. another verb + prepositional phrase
_____ 3. noun + prepositional phrase
_____ 4. prepositional phrase at the beginning of a sentence
_____ 5. prepositional phrase at the end of a sentence

EXAMPLES

a. In the future, I hope to visit the Galápagos Islands.
b. The Galápagos Islands are <u>in the Pacific Ocean</u>.
c. Many visitors travel to the Galápagos to see the animals there.
d. The animals in the Galápagos are very unusual.
e. The animals are protected and safe on these islands.

TRY IT OUT! Work alone or with a partner. Combine each group of sentences into one sentence with prepositional phrases. There is more than one way to form each sentence.

1. There are beaches. They are near my hometown. They are beautiful.

   Near my hometown, there are beautiful beaches.

2. I go to the beach. I go there with my friends. I go there on weekends.

   _____

3. There are many hotels. They are for tourists. The hotels are in my hometown.

   _____

4. Tourists come to relax. They are from other countries. They come to my hometown.

   _____

5. There are good restaurants. They are on the main street. The street is in my neighborhood.

   _____

6. There are free concerts. They are in the park. They are in the summer.

   _____

✎ Applying Vocabulary: Using Words for Directions

You will need to use direction words when you write about your hometown on page 103. Review the direction words you learned on page 91. Then read about how to use direction words in sentences.

RULES	EXAMPLES
1. Use *north/south/east/west* + *of* + a place.	Costa Rica is south **of Nicaragua**. Belize is northeast **of Guatemala**.
2. Add *-ern* to a direction word to form an adjective.	My hometown is in **southern** Japan. I come from the **northwestern** part of Morocco.
3. Use a capital letter for a direction word only when the word is a name or part of a name.	The state of South Carolina is in the southeastern part of the United States. The state of Oregon is in the Northwest.

PRACTICE 9 Using Direction Words

Work alone or with a partner. Look at the map. Write one or more sentences about the location of each place in parentheses. Use direction words.

1. (Turkey) _____

2. (Ankara) _____

3. (Istanbul) _____

4. (Antalya) _____

TRY IT OUT! Interview two or more of your classmates. Find out where they are from. On a sheet of paper, write sentences about these classmates. Use direction words.

Gustavo is from Recife. It is in the eastern part of Brazil. It is about 1,400 miles north of Rio de Janeiro.

You are going to write a paragraph about your hometown, like the writing models on pages 89 and 90. First, you will **brainstorm**. Brainstorming is a way of getting ideas. It means thinking about a topic and quickly writing down all the thoughts that come to mind. After you brainstorm, you will choose some of the ideas to use in your paragraph.

Prewrite ⟩ **STEP 1: Prewrite to get ideas.**

a. Get ready to write by brainstorming about your hometown. Quickly make a list of all the ideas that come to mind.

- Do not write complete sentences. Just take notes.
- Do not worry about whether an idea is good or bad. You will decide later which ideas you do and do not want to use.
- Do not worry about the order of your ideas. You will put them in order later.

Here are the notes from one student's brainstorming:

in Kazakhstan, in the southeast, near China (how far?)
big city—population??   noisy (but I like)
public transportation good
some beautiful buildings   culture!
mountains, beautiful nature, snow
Medeo—high in mountains, rink for speed skating—famous
expensive city   was capital city (dates?)
name = "the apple place"

Now brainstorm about your hometown. Take notes.

b. Work with a partner. Ask your partner questions about his or her hometown, questions such as:
- Where are you from?
- Where is it?
- What is it like?
- What is special about it?

Answer your partner's questions about your hometown. As you get more ideas, add them to your notes.

c. Look again at the brainstorming notes from page 103. The writer has made changes. She has decided on a title. She has written a topic sentence. She has crossed out information she does not plan to use.

Almaty

topic sentence: Almaty, my hometown, is a special city.

in Kazakhstan, in the southeast, near China ~~(how far?)~~

~~big city—population??~~   ~~noisy (but I like)~~

~~public transportation good~~

some beautiful buildings   culture! (theaters, museums)

mountains, beautiful nature, snow

Medeo—high in mountains, rink for speed skating—famous, world's largest

~~expensive city~~   was capital city ~~(dates?)~~

name = "the apple place"   Kazakhstan famous for apples,
                          first apples in the world

 Write

STEP 2: Write the first draft.

a. Review your notes to prepare for writing your first draft. Decide what information you do and do not want to use.

b. Write your first draft. Begin your paragraph with a topic sentence. See the writing models on pages 89 and 90 for examples. Remember that your supporting sentences must relate to your topic sentence.

Writing Tip

Prewriting often helps a writer decide on a topic sentence. However, some writers like to write their first draft of a paragraph without a topic sentence. Then they add it afterwards. Remember that you can change your topic sentence when you revise and edit.

 **Edit**

STEP 3: Revise and edit the draft.

a. Read your paragraph again. It may help you to read it out loud. Make changes if needed.

b. Do peer review. Sit with a partner and exchange papers. Give each other feedback. Follow the steps on the Peer Review Worksheet.

PEER REVIEW WORKSHEET

Your partner's name: _____

Content

1. Read all of your partner's paragraph.

2. Underline any part of the paragraph you do not understand. Ask your partner to explain it.

3. Circle the topic sentence. If there is no topic sentence, write *TS?* on the paper.

4. Read the supporting sentences again. Ask questions if you want more information.

Format and Language

5. Use this list to check your partner's paper. Mark any problems on the paper in pencil. Check (✓) each item in the list as you finish.

   ☐ the format of the paper—heading, title, margins, spacing
   ☐ a subject in every sentence
   ☐ a verb for every subject
   ☐ the use of *there is* and *there are*
   ☐ the use of prepositions

6. Put a question mark (?) if you are not sure about something.

---

c. Return your partner's paper. Can you say something nice about it?

d. Look at your own paper. If you do not agree with the feedback, then ask another student or your teacher. Mark any changes you want to make.

Writing Tip

Help yourself do a better job of revising and editing by giving yourself time. Take a break before you start on a new draft. Work on something else for a while, or better yet, get a good night's sleep. Then go back to your paragraph with fresh eyes.

Write **STEP 4: Write a new draft.**

a. Take a new sheet of paper and write a new draft.

b. Edit your new draft carefully. Then hand it in to your teacher.

SELF-ASSESSMENT

In this chapter, you learned to:
○ Identify and write supporting sentences
○ Use the articles *a*, *an*, and *the* with nouns
○ Write sentences with *there is* and *there are*
○ Use prepositional phrases to describe locations
○ Write, revise, and edit a paragraph about your hometown

Which ones can you do well? Mark them ☑

Which ones do you need to practice more? Mark them ⊗

EXPANSION

 ## ON YOUR OWN

Write a paragraph about a favorite place. For example, you could describe your favorite room at home or a place where you go on vacation. Before you begin, brainstorm about the place and take notes.

Use your notes to write your first draft. Your paragraph must have a topic sentence. All the supporting sentences should relate to your main idea.

Ask a friend or a classmate to review your first draft. Use the Peer Review Worksheet on page 105. Then prepare a new draft and give it to your teacher.

 ## YOUR JOURNAL

Continue making entries in your journal. If you cannot think of a topic for a journal entry, try one of these ideas:

- Do you ever watch the sun come up or watch it set? Describe a place where you like to watch the sunrise or sunset.

- Do you carry a wallet, a purse, or a backpack? Describe what is in it right now.

- Write about using English outside of class. Who do you talk to in English? When do you listen to English or read it?

For more ideas for journal entries, see Appendix A on page 193.

CHAPTER 6

ON THE JOB

OBJECTIVES

Writers need certain skills.

In this chapter, you will learn to:

- Make sure that supporting sentences are relevant
- Use present progressive verbs in sentences
- Recognize and use non-action verbs
- Use *have* as an action verb and as a non-action verb
- Choose between the simple present and present progressive
- Write simple sentences with different sentence patterns
- Write, revise, and edit a paragraph about someone at work

In a meeting

On a construction site

In this chapter, you will see many photos of people at their jobs. You will choose a photo of someone at work, and you will write a paragraph about what the person is doing in the photo and what his or her usual job **responsibilities** are—the things that he or she has to do at work.

LOOKING AT THE MODELS

In each writing model, the writer describes someone in a photo. The photo shows the person at work. The writer tells both what the person is doing in the photo and what the person usually does on the job.

Work with a partner or in a small group. Look at the photos. Read the models. Then answer the questions.

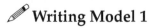 **Writing Model 1**

A Baker at Work

The man in Photo 1 is a baker. He has a good job, but it is hard work. He starts work at 4:00 A.M. He works long hours and never sits down. He makes many kinds of bread and pastries. In this photo, the baker is standing in the kitchen of the bakery. He is wearing a white jacket and a white apron. Behind him, there are many trays of baked goods. He is holding two pieces of bread and smiling. He feels proud of his work.

Photo 1

Questions about the Model

1. **a.** What is the topic of the paragraph?

_____

   b. What is the writer's controlling idea about the topic?

_____

2. What details does the writer give in the paragraph? Check (✓) your answers.

☐ what the man's job is   ☐ his feelings about his work

☐ where he is   ☐ how much money he earns

☐ things that you can see in the photo   ☐ what he is doing at this moment

☐ the man's clothing   ☐ what he does every day

3. Would you like to have this man's job? Circle your answer: *(Yes / No)* Explain your answer to your partner or group.

4. What **simple present** verbs does the writer use? Fill in the blanks.

a. He _____ work at 4:00 A.M.

b. He _____ long hours and never _____ down.

c. He _____ proud of his work.

5. What **present progressive** verbs does the writer use? Fill in the blanks.

a. In this photo, the baker _____ in the kitchen of the bakery.

b. He _____ a white jacket and a white apron.

c. He _____ two pieces of bread and _____ .

✎ **Writing Model 2**

The Job of a Pharmacist

Photo 2 shows a pharmacist at work. She has a very responsible job. In this photo, she is standing at a counter in the pharmacy. She is holding a bottle of medicine and is wearing a white lab coat. She is listening to someone on the phone. She looks serious. Maybe a customer is having a problem with a prescription. Every day, the pharmacist talks to customers about their prescriptions. She answers their questions on the phone and at the counter. She has to give them the right medicine and the right information. She sometimes needs to talk to doctors or nurses about the prescriptions. People depend on her. A pharmacist has a lot of responsibility.

Photo 2

(continued on next page)

Questions about the Model

1. a. What is the topic of the paragraph?

_____

b. What is the writer's controlling idea about the topic?

_____

2. What details does the writer give in the paragraph? Check (✓) your answers.

☐ what the woman's job is   ☐ her feelings about her work

☐ where she is   ☐ how much money she earns

☐ things that you can see in   ☐ what she is doing at
   the photo   this moment

☐ the woman's clothing   ☐ what she does every day

3. Would you like to have this woman's job? Circle your answer: _(Yes / No)_ Explain your answer to your partner or group.

4. What does the verb _look_ mean in these two sentences from the model? Write the number of the meaning, _1_ or _2_.
(1) seem, appear   (2) turn your eyes to see someone or something

_____ **a.** She is holding a bottle of medicine and **looking** at her computer screen.

_____ **b.** She **looks** serious.

✎ Looking at Vocabulary: Words for Jobs

Many words for jobs end in _-er_ or _-or_, such as _teacher_ (a person who teaches) or _machine operator_ (a person who operates a machine in a factory). Another common ending is _-ist_, as in _scientist_ (a person who works in science). There are also many words for jobs that do not use any of these endings, such as _salesperson_ and _musician_.

PRACTICE 1   Words for Jobs

Ⓐ Find four words for jobs in the writing models. Fill in the blanks.

1. A word that ends in _-er_: _____

2. A word that ends in _-or_: _____

3. A word that ends in _-ist_: _____

4. A word without a special ending: _____

B Complete the chart with the job words from the box. Then check (✓) the words you know. Learn the meanings of the other words by using a dictionary or asking someone.

~~actor~~	firefighter	~~pilot~~	reporter
author	hair stylist	professor	veterinarian
dentist	mechanic	receptionist	waiter

-ER	-OR	-IST	OTHER WORDS
	actor		pilot

ORGANIZATION

SUPPORTING SENTENCES, PART 2

Support for the Topic Sentence

In Chapter 3, you learned about topic sentences. In Chapter 5, you learned about supporting sentences. They form the body of a paragraph—the middle of the paragraph and its largest part.

Supporting sentences must show why the topic sentence is true. They must present **evidence**—information that helps to prove the writer's point about the topic.

PRACTICE 2   Supporting Sentences

Work alone or with a partner. Read each topic sentence. Circle the topic and underline the controlling idea. Write two supporting sentences.

1. (Doctors) need good communication skills.

    a.   _They need to be good listeners._

    b.   _They need to give clear explanations to their patients._

2. Hawaii is a great place for a vacation.

    a.   _____

    b.   _____

(continued on next page)

3. There are several reasons I go to the gym.

a. _____

b. _____

4. Movies are more fun in a movie theater.

a. _____

b. _____

5. A good education is valuable for many reasons.

a. _____

b. _____

6. A pilot has a lot of responsibility.

a. _____

b. _____

PARAGRAPH UNITY

A good paragraph must have **unity**. That means that all the supporting sentences in a paragraph must be **relevant**—they must relate to the controlling idea in the topic sentence. The opposite of *relevant* is *irrelevant*. A sentence that goes off-topic or does not support the controlling idea is irrelevant, and it does not belong in the paragraph.

In this paragraph, two irrelevant sentences are crossed out.

Being a Professional Baseball Player

Professional baseball players have a high-pressure job. When they are at work, thousands of people are watching them. They know many people will see any mistakes they make. ~~Baseball fans feel pressure, too.~~ When it is their turn at bat, baseball players know that their team is depending on them to get a hit. That means more pressure. They also know that they have to play well, or the team manager will take them out of the game. Professional baseball players must be able to play well under pressure. ~~Good players make good money.~~

The topic of the paragraph is the job of professional baseball players. The controlling idea is that they have a high-pressure job. The two crossed-out sentences do not explain why his job is high pressure.

- The sentence about the fans is about their feelings, not the players'. It does not support the controlling idea, so it is irrelevant in this paragraph.
- The sentence about good players making a lot of money is true, but it, too, is irrelevant in this paragraph because it does not support the controlling idea.

PRACTICE 3   Identifying Irrelevant Sentences

Work alone or with a partner. Read each paragraph. Underline the topic sentence. Find two irrelevant sentences, and cross them out.

PARAGRAPH 1

The Job of a Chef

Chefs need to be very organized. They are responsible for managing the kitchens of busy restaurants and hotels. They often direct the work of many other people. Some chefs are really bad bosses. They want their kitchens to be well-organized, with everything in its place and everyone working as a team. Many chefs like to invent new dishes. Chefs need to do a lot of planning. For example, they need to plan menus and order supplies. All these responsibilities require good organizational skills.

PARAGRAPH 2

Conditions in Antarctica

Antarctica is a difficult and dangerous place for people. Penguins live there. It is very cold, with the average temperature about 40 degrees below zero. The air is very dry, and there are strong winds. In the winter, the sun never comes up. I would never go there in the winter. In the summer, the strong rays of the sun are bad for people's skin and eyes. They need protection from both the cold and the sun. Some people stay in Antarctica for a few days, weeks, or months, but no one calls Antarctica home.

(continued on next page)

My Favorite Holiday

I always loved the traditions of New Year's Eve in my country. First, we all cleaned our homes so they looked nice for the new year. We also put up colored lights and other decorations. Then everyone dressed up in nice new clothes. My brother never wanted to help with the cleaning or get dressed up. The best tradition was a special dinner with all our relatives. Then at midnight, everyone went outside, and there were fireworks in the streets. Sometimes we had fireworks on other holidays, too. I always loved celebrating the new year in my country.

GRAMMAR

THE PRESENT PROGRESSIVE

In Chapters 2 and 3, you learned about verbs in the simple present tense. Now you will learn about verbs in the **present progressive** (also called the *present continuous*).

A present progressive verb has two parts:

(1) the verb *be*: *am*, *is*, or *are*

(2) a **main verb** that ends in *-ing*.

    (1)   (2)
Excuse me, my phone **is** ringing.

Present Progressive Verb Forms

SINGULAR				PLURAL			
Subject	**Be**	**(Not)**	**Main Verb**	**Subject**	**Be**	**(Not)**	**Main Verb**
I	am			We			
You	are			You	are	(not)	working.
He		(not)	working.	They			
She	is						
It							

See Appendix C3, page 199, for contractions with am, is, *and* are.

See Appendix C5, page 205, for spelling rules for verbs ending in -ing.

Describing Actions

Ⓐ Match the verbs with the pictures. Write a sentence for each picture using the present progressive form of the verb.

a. drive **c.** listen **e.** fix **g.** stand

~~**b.** use~~ **d.** run **f.** hold **h.** carry

___b___ **1.**

He is using a computer.

_____ **2.**

_____

_____ **3.**

_____

_____ **4.**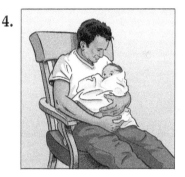

_____

_____ **5.**

_____

_____ **6.**

_____

_____ **7.**

_____

_____ **8.**

_____

B What are you doing right now? Write two or more sentences. Use the present progressive.

_____

_____

TRY IT OUT!   Take a sheet of paper. Write four or more statements about the people in each picture. Use the present progressive to tell what is happening. Write both affirmative and negative statements.

Picture A: *The people are waiting for a bus. The two men are not talking.*

Picture A   *Picture B*

PRESENT PROGRESSIVE VS. SIMPLE PRESENT

Verb Functions

Compare the uses of the present progressive and the simple present.

Present progressive

The present progressive is used to describe actions happening at this moment. For example:

You **are reading** this sentence.

The present progressive is also used to describe actions happening over a longer time period. The period continues in the present. For example:

Habiba **is taking** a math course this semester.

The scientists **are working** in Antarctica for a few weeks.

Simple present

The simple present is used to state facts and to describe routines and habits—actions that happen again and again. For example:

The sun **rises** in the east.

I **eat** breakfast at home.

Because the present progressive and the simple present have different meanings, they are used with different time expressions. Study the rules and examples in the chart.

RULES	EXAMPLES
1. Use the present progressive with time expressions such as: • *now, right now*, and *at this moment* • *this week, this month, this year*	You are reading **right now**. She is studying English **this year**.
2. Do not use the present progressive with adverbs of frequency. Use the simple present.	*go* **Sometimes** I ~~am going~~ to the movies on weekends.

PRACTICE 5   Present Progressive vs. Simple Present

Fill in the blanks. Use the present progressive or simple present form of the verb in parentheses.

1. (fix) The mechanic _____ my car now. Every day, he

a.

   _____ cars with many different kinds of problems.

b.

2. (write) Sometimes my doctor _____ prescriptions. At

a.

   this moment, she _____ a prescription for me.

b.

3. (work) Veterinarians often _____ with different kinds

a.

   of animals, but Dr. Garcia always _____ with horses.

b.

4. (teach) Lindsay is an English professor. At the moment, she

   _____ a class in the writing lab. This semester, she

a.

   _____ three courses.

b.

5. (talk) My cousin is a receptionist in a doctor's office. She

   _____ to everyone who comes into the office. She

a.

   _____ to patients all day every day.

b.

(continued on next page)

6. (learn) Edward is going to school to become a hair stylist. He

_____ to cut people's hair. This week, he and his
    a.

classmates _____ how to cut short hair on men.
    b.

7. (travel) Jack _____ this week. He
    a.

_____ every week for his job. He is a sales rep for a
    b.

toy company.

Non-Action Verbs

Some verbs do not express action or movement. These verbs are called
non-action verbs (or *stative* verbs). Do not use the present progressive with
non-action verbs. Use the simple present.

> do not like   prefer
> I ~~am not liking~~ coffee. I ~~am preferring~~ tea.

The verbs in the chart are also non-action verbs like *prefer* and *like*.
Remember to use only simple present forms of these verbs.

NON-ACTION VERBS			
Description	**Senses**	**Mental States**	**Emotions**
be	hear	know	hate
look*	see	need	dislike
seem	smell	want	love

look = seem or appear to be: *She looks sad. Look* is an action verb when it means "turn your eyes to see."

PRACTICE 6   Action vs. Non-Action Verbs

Circle the correct verb.

1. This pizza tastes great. I *(am liking / like)* it!

2. Please be quiet. You *(are making / make)* too much noise.

3. I do not understand this homework. I *(am needing / need)* some help.

4. The students always *(are looking / look)* sleepy on Monday mornings.

5. Beatriz is at the mall. She *(is looking for / looks for)* a new dress.

6. Nanami has her radio on. She *(is listening / listens)* to the news at the moment.

7. Listen! Do you hear music?—No, I *(am not hearing / do not hear)* anything.

8. Tom is at the pharmacy. He *(is wanting / wants)* some cold medicine.

The Verb *Have*

The verb *have* can be an **action verb** or a **non-action verb**. It depends on the meaning of *have* in the sentence.

RULES	EXAMPLES
1. *Have* is an action verb when it means: • eating or drinking • doing or experiencing something You can use either the present progressive or the simple present.	He is having lunch now. He always has lunch at noon. They are having a party. It's noisy! They often have loud parties.

2. *Have* is a non-action verb when it refers to:
• possession
• relationship
• sickness
 	
Do not use the present progressive. Use the simple present.
	She has **a new car**.
	
	He does not have **any brothers**.
	
	I have **a headache**.
	
	NOT: She ~~is having~~ a new car.
	    He ~~is not having~~ any brothers.
	    I ~~am having~~ a headache.

PRACTICE 7   Action vs. Non-Action with *Have*

Circle the correct verb.

1. Slava likes animals, but he *(is not having / does not have)* a pet.

2. Mr. Brown is out of the office right now. He *(is having / has)* lunch.

3. My sister *(is having / has)* two children, one boy and one girl.

4. My head hurts, and I *(am having / have)* a sore throat.

5. Monique *(is not having / does not have)* a good job.

6. My friends are at a party now. I am sure they *(are having / have)* fun.

7. I am drinking tea, and she *(is having / has)* coffee.

8. Students often *(are having / have)* exams at the end of the school year.

Find eight more verb errors in the paragraph. Make corrections.

1 Danny ~~is wanting~~ *wants* to buy a car. 2 He is having a new job and needing a car for work. 3 Right now, he is at Ace Used Cars. 4 He is looking at a car. 5 A salesperson is talk to Danny. 6 She describing the car to him. 7 He listens to her. 8 The car is not bad, but Danny is not liking it very much. 9 He is want a nice car, but he is not have much money. 10 The price for this car seems right. 11 He is thinking about it.

SENTENCE STRUCTURE

SIMPLE SENTENCE PATTERNS, PART 2

In Chapter 4, you learned that simple sentences have one subject-verb combination. You saw simple sentences with these two patterns:

1 subject + **1** verb	I work in a factory.
2 subjects + **1** verb	Mark and I work in the same factory.

Here are two more patterns for simple sentences. These patterns also have one subject-verb combination.

1 subject + **2** verbs	Stan sits and works in an office all day.
	Stan is sitting and working now.
2 subjects + **2** verbs	Stan and Lisa sit and work in an office all day.

Study the rules and examples in the chart.

RULES	EXAMPLES
1. Use *and* to add a second subject or a second verb. Do not use a comma.	Doctors **and** nurses work in hospitals. They examine **and** treat patients.
2. Use *or* to connect two negative verbs.	Nurses' aides do not examine **or** treat patients.
3. When you connect two verbs, do not repeat *do/does not* or *am/is/are not*.	My doctor is on vacation, so he is not taking calls **or** ~~is not~~ replying to email.

PRACTICE 9   Recognizing Simple Sentence Patterns

Work alone or with a partner. Underline the verbs and write *V* above them. Underline the subjects and write *S* above them.

1. Eva exercises and eats healthy food.

2. She takes vitamins and gets plenty of sleep.

3. She eats fresh vegetables and avoids fast food.

4. Her parents and her brother also eat well and exercise.

5. Eva and her brother work out six days a week.

6. She walks on a treadmill and rides an exercise bicycle.

7. She does not lift weights or run.

8. Eva and her brother look good and feel great.

She is on a treadmill.

He is lifting weights.

Ⓐ Combine each pair of sentences into one simple sentence. Use *and* or *or* to connect the present progressive verbs.

1. The bus driver is not listening to music. He is not talking to the passengers.

   The bus driver is not listening to music or talking to the passengers.

2. The players are putting on their uniforms. They are getting ready for the game.

   _____

3. The security guard is not watching TV. He is not sleeping on the job.

   _____

4. The teacher is sitting at his desk. He is correcting students' papers.

   _____

5. The fashion model is not smiling. She is not speaking to the photographer.

   _____

Ⓑ Combine each pair of sentences into one simple sentence. Use *and* to connect two subjects. Use *and* or *or* to connect the simple present verbs.

1. Police officers wear uniforms. Soldiers wear uniforms.

   Police officers and soldiers wear uniforms.

2. A dentist examines people's teeth. A dentist fixes tooth problems.

   _____

3. Computer technicians understand computers. Computer technicians fix computer problems.

   _____

4. Farmers do not sleep late. Farmers do not take many days off.

   _____

5. Cooks work in kitchens. They prepare food. Bakers work in kitchens. They prepare food.

   _____

Writing Tip

Make your writing more interesting by using a variety of sentence patterns. When you revise a paragraph, try combining short sentences.

✏️ **Applying Vocabulary: Using Words for Jobs**

You will need to use words for jobs when you speak and write about the people in the photos on page 125. Review the words for jobs on pages 110 and 111, such as *baker* and *pharmacist*.

You have seen many other words for jobs in this chapter. Practice 11 will let you test your memory of words for jobs and discuss job responsibilities.

PRACTICE 11   Words for Jobs

Ⓐ Complete the sentences. Check your answers by looking at the list of words in Part B on the next page.

1. A person who fixes problems with computers is a

   _____*computer technician*_____ .

2. A person whose job is to stop fires is a _____ .

3. A person whose job is to repair cars or other machines is a

   _____ .

4. A person who works with doctors to take care of sick or injured people

   is a _____ .

5. A person who operates the controls of an airplane or helicopter

   is a _____ .

6. A person whose job is to report the news in a newspaper or on TV, radio,

   or the Internet is a _____ .

7. A person whose job is to give medical care to sick or injured animals

   is a _____ .

8. A man who serves food in a restaurant is a _____ .

A computer technician

B Work with a partner. Complete the statements with words from the box. There is more than one way to complete each statement.

computer technicians	mechanics	pilots	veterinarians
firefighters	nurses	reporters	waiters

EXAMPLE

_____Nurses_____ help in emergencies.

1. _____ help in emergencies.

2. _____ fix machines.

3. _____ wear uniforms.

4. _____ interview people.

5. _____ need good communication skills.

6. _____ use computers at work.

WRITING ASSIGNMENT

You are going to write a paragraph about a person in a photo, like the writing models on pages 108 and 109. Your paragraph will describe both the person's job and what the person is doing at this moment in the photo.

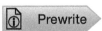 Prewrite

STEP 1: Prewrite to get ideas.

a. Choose one of the four photos to write about.

b. Work with a partner who has chosen a different photo. Tell your partner about the person in your photo. Talk about:
   - what the person's job is
   - what you think about this job
   - what the person usually does at work
   - where the person is at this moment
   - what the person is doing now
   - what the person is wearing
   - how the person feels and why

c. Take notes about your photo on a sheet of paper.

> **Writing Tip**
>
> When you are planning to write a paragraph, it is natural to think about the topic in your first language. But you also need to ask yourself, "What can I say about this topic in English?" Be sure to choose a topic that is a good match for your English writing skills.

Photo 1

Photo 2

Photo 3

Photo 4

 Write

STEP 2: Write the first draft.

a. Use your notes to write the first draft of a paragraph. At the beginning of your paragraph:

- Identify which photo you are writing about.
- Write a topic sentence.

Look at the writing models on pages 108 and 109 for examples.

(continued on next page)

You can use an adjective to express the controlling idea about your topic.

He has an **interesting** job.

Her job is sometimes **difficult**.

Here are some other adjectives that can describe jobs: *boring, easy, exciting, great, important, satisfying,* and *stressful.*

b. Continue writing your first draft. Make sure that your supporting sentences about the person's job show why your controlling idea is true.

c. Give your paragraph a title.

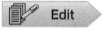 **Edit**

STEP 3: Revise and edit the first draft.

a. Read your paragraph again. It may help you to read it out loud. Make changes if needed. Check for mistakes. Cross out any irrelevant sentences.

b. Do peer review. Sit with a partner and exchange papers. Give each other feedback. Follow the steps on the Peer Review Worksheet.

PEER REVIEW WORKSHEET

Your partner's name: _____

Content

1. Read all of your partner's paragraph.

2. Underline any part of the paragraph you do not understand. Ask your partner to explain it.

3. Circle the writer's controlling idea about the topic.

4. Ask about any sentences in the paragraph that do not seem relevant.

5. Ask questions if you want more information about the person in the photo.

Format and Language

6. Use this list to check your partner's paper. Mark any problems on the paper in pencil. Check (✓) each item in the list as you finish.

   ☐ a subject in every sentence   ☐ the use of simple present verbs
   ☐ a verb for every subject   ☐ the use of present progressive verbs

7. Put a question mark (?) if you are not sure about something.

---

c. Return your partner's paper. Can you say something nice about it?

d. Look at your own paper. If you do not agree with the feedback on it, ask another student or your teacher. Mark any changes you want to make.

 **Write** | **STEP 4: Write a new draft.**

    a. Take a new sheet of paper, and write a new draft.

    b. Check your paragraph carefully. Then hand it in to your teacher.

SELF-ASSESSMENT

In this chapter, you learned to:

- ○ Make sure supporting sentences are relevant
- ○ Use present progressive verbs in sentences
- ○ Recognize and use non-action verbs
- ○ Use *have* as both an action verb and a non-action verb
- ○ Choose between the simple present and present progressive
- ○ Write simple sentences with different sentence patterns
- ○ Write, revise, and edit a paragraph about someone at work

Which ones can you do well? Mark them ✓

Which ones do you need to practice more? Mark them ✗

EXPANSION

 ## TIMED WRITING

Students need to write quickly to succeed in academic writing. For example, sometimes students need to do a writing assignment in class or on a test, and they have only a short time to do it.

To practice writing quickly, you are going to write a paragraph in class. You will have 20 minutes. To complete the assignment in time, follow these steps.

1. Read the writing prompt on page 128 (or the prompt that your teacher gives you). Make sure that you understand the prompt. If you have questions, ask your teacher. (2 minutes)

2. Brainstorm to get ideas. On a sheet of paper, make some notes. Then think about organizing your ideas. Mark up your notes with circles, arrows, and numbers to show the order of information in your paragraph. Write a topic sentence for your paragraph. (6 minutes)

3. Write your paragraph. Be sure to include a topic sentence and supporting sentences. (10 minutes)

(continued on next page)

4. Check your paragraph. Correct any mistakes. (2 minutes)

5. Give your paper to your teacher.

Prompt: Write a paragraph about a person who has a good job. You can write about someone you know ("My uncle has a good job.") or about anyone who does a certain kind of job ("A news photographer has a good job."). Write what makes the job a good one.

 ## YOUR JOURNAL

Continue making entries in your journal. If you cannot think of a topic for a journal entry, try one of these ideas.

- Where are you at this moment? Describe what you are doing and what you are wearing. Are there any other people around you? Tell what they are doing.

- Name a job that interests you, one that you might like to do in the future. Why are you interested in this job?

- These days, you are going to classes and you are using this book. What else are you doing—in and outside of school— to learn English? What helps you the most?

For more ideas for journal entries, see Appendix A on page 193.

CHAPTER 7

REMEMBERING AN IMPORTANT EVENT

OBJECTIVES

Writers need certain skills.

In this chapter, you will learn to:

- Organize your ideas during prewriting
- Write compound sentences with *and*, *but*, and *so*
- Apply rules for using commas in sentences
- Use simple past verbs
- Write, revise, and edit a paragraph about an important event in your life

A big day

In this chapter, you will be reading about people's memories of important **events** in their lives. An event is something that happens, especially something important, interesting, or unusual. You will write a paragraph to share your memories of an important event or a special day in your own life.

LOOKING AT THE MODELS

In the writing models, two students describe special events in their lives.

Work with a partner or in a small group. Read the models. Then answer the questions.

✎ Writing Model 1

An Important Day in My Life

The day of my high school graduation was a good day for me. It was a Saturday. In the morning, I got dressed. I had a new suit and tie for that day. Then I went to a friend's house. Six of my friends were there. Later, we rode to the school together in my friend's car. At 2:00 P.M., all the students in my class entered the school gymnasium. My parents and grandparents were already in their seats, and they took a lot of pictures. The principal called the names of the honor students first. I was in that group, and I won a prize because I was the best math student. I was very happy about that, and my family was proud of me that day.

Questions about the Model

1. What is the topic sentence? Circle the topic and underline the controlling idea.

2. Why was it a good day for the writer? Give one reason.

   _____

3. What details does the writer include in his description of the day?

   ☐ the weather   ☐ places he went

   ☐ other people   ☐ things he did

   ☐ his clothing   ☐ his feelings

4. What are some words and phrases that show the writer is using time order?

_____

5. What **simple past** forms of the verb *be* did the writer use? Fill in the blanks.

   a. It _____ a Saturday.

   b. Six of my friends _____ there.

6. What simple past forms of **regular verbs** did the writer use?

   a. At 2:00 P.M., the students in my class _____ the gymnasium.

   b. The principal _____ the names of the honor students first.

7. What simple past forms of **irregular verbs** did the writer use?

   a. In the morning, I _____ dressed.

   b. I _____ a new suit and tie for that day.

   c. Then I _____ to a friend's house.

✎ **Writing Model 2**

ı ı ⊻ ı ı ı ı ı ı 1 ı ı ı ı ı ı 2 ı ı ı ı ı 3 ı ı ı ı ı 4 ı ı ı ı ı 5 ı ı ı ı ı 6 △ ı ı

My Wedding Day

I have many wonderful memories of my wedding day. I would like to tell you about three of them. First of all, I remember the beautiful weather. The week before was cold and cloudy, but my wedding day was sunny and warm. I felt lucky. I also remember seeing smiles all around me that day. Almost 100 of my relatives and friends were there. They liked my future husband, so they were happy for me. Most of all, I remember walking up the aisle with him after the ceremony. I carried a bouquet of yellow flowers, and I held his arm tightly. My heart was very full. This unforgettable day began a new life for me.

Questions about the Model

1. What is the topic of the paragraph? _____

2. What is the controlling idea about the topic?

_____

(continued on next page)

3. What three memories of her wedding day does the writer focus on? Check (✓) your answers.

☐ the weather   ☐ the place she got married

☐ the music   ☐ how she looked

☐ the people at her wedding   ☐ how she felt

4. What adjective means "impossible to forget"? _____

5. What **coordinating conjunctions** did the writer use? Fill in the blanks.

   a. The week before was cloudy, _____ my wedding day was sunny and warm.

   b. They liked my husband, _____ they were happy for me.

   c. I carried a bouquet of yellow flowers, _____ I held his arm tightly.

Looking at Vocabulary: Adjectives + Prepositions

Sometimes an adjective is followed by a prepositional phrase, as in . . . *they were happy for me* (from Writing Model 2). Some adjectives always take the same preposition. Other adjectives can take more than one preposition.

Use *happy + for +* a person: I was **happy for** my friend when he won first prize.

Use *happy + about +* a thing, idea, or event: I was **happy about** my grade.

PRACTICE 1   Adjectives + Prepositions

Ⓐ Find the adjectives *happy* and *proud* in Writing Model 1 and *happy* in Writing Model 2. Circle the prepositions that follow them.

Ⓑ Fill in the blanks. Use the adjective + preposition combinations from the box. There is more than one way to complete each statement.

afraid of	good at	nervous about
excited about	interested in	proud of

1. I was _____ getting married.

2. I was always _____ sports.

3. My parents were _____ me.

4. I was _____ getting lost.

5. I was _____ the changes in my life.

6. I was _____ making decisions.

ORGANIZING YOUR IDEAS

The information in a paragraph needs to be organized. The writer must put the information in some kind of order. This makes the paragraph easier to read and understand.

There are many ways to organize a paragraph. For example, you can use time order. You studied time order in Chapter 4, and the author of Writing Model 1 in this chapter used time order for his paragraph. Writing Model 2, however, is different. The writer used **listing order**. When using listing order, the writer divides the topic into separate points and then discusses them one by one.

Writers need to make some decisions about organization early in the writing process, during prewriting. Read about how the two writers did their prewriting and organized their ideas.

Getting Organized: Time Order

For a prewriting activity, the author of Writing Model 1 made a list of notes about the day. He wrote the list in time order.

> got up
> had breakfast
> made phone calls
> got dressed—new clothes
> T's house—6 friends
> driving around town, then to school
> walking into the gym with my class
> parents, grandparents, pictures
> honor students first, my prize
> dinner at restaurant
> parties

The writer needed to limit his paragraph. He had to decide what information from his list to keep and what information to leave out.

PRACTICE 2   Choosing Ideas from Prewriting

Work alone or with a partner. Reread Writing Model 1 on page 130. In the list of notes above, underline the details that the writer chose to use in his paragraph. Cross out the notes the writer did not use.

Getting Organized: Listing Order

As a prewriting activity, the author of Writing Model 2 tried **freewriting**. Freewriting means writing about a topic for five or ten minutes without stopping.

The author of Writing Model 2 wrote quickly, keeping her fingers moving on the keyboard. She did not worry about mistakes in spelling or grammar. She did not worry about writing incomplete sentences or repeating ideas. She thought only about getting her ideas out as fast as possible. That is the goal of freewriting.

My Wedding Day

my wedding day, one of most important days of my life, I have many things to say. exciting, wonderful day. the day beautiful, warm sun, a surprise, not like before. it was october, a saturday. in the early morning, I woke up before the ring of my alarm clock. I was excited. I start to get ready, doing my hair, my dress, what will I say about my dress? my sisters and my friends in my room helping me. at the church,  I remember flowers and music, singing, piano. feeling love around me. many friends, relatives, almost 100, I see their faces, everybody smiling and smiling, so happy for me. my mother and father's faces, tears, smiling. I see my future husband, our eyes meeting. about the wedding, what can I say, the (name?) talking, he gave much good advice to us. I walked (how to say?) with my husband, I remember walking slowly, holding his arm, so happy. beginning of our new life together.

Page 1   Sec 1   1/1

The writer needed to limit her paragraph. She could not use all the ideas in her freewriting. She had to decide what to keep and what to leave out.

After looking at her freewriting, the writer decided to use listing order for her paragraph. She decided on three important memories of her wedding day: the lovely weather, the smiles of her friends and relatives, and the walk up the aisle with her husband after the ceremony. Then she chose details to support each point, to explain why each of these memories was important to her.

You will see that in the final paragraph, she also added some details that were not in her freewriting.

PRACTICE 3   **Choosing Ideas from Prewriting**

Work alone or with a partner. Reread Writing Model 2 on page 131. Then look at the writer's freewriting on page 134. Underline the parts of her freewriting that she decided to use for her paragraph. Cross out the ideas the writer did not use.

PRACTICE 4   **Listing Order and Supporting Sentences**

A Look again at Writing Model 2 on page 131. Put a check (✓) before each sentence that introduces a key memory of the writer's wedding day. Underline the six sentences that give details.

B Compare Writing Model 2 with the writer's freewriting on page 134. Look for details in the writing model that were not in the freewriting. Double underline those new details in the writing model.

SENTENCE STRUCTURE AND MECHANICS

SIMPLE VS. COMPOUND SENTENCES

Review of Simple Sentences

In Chapters 4 and 6, you studied four patterns for simple sentences. Each pattern has one subject-verb combination.

1 SUBJECT + **1** VERB
I watched the World Cup.

2 SUBJECTS + **1** VERB
My friends and I watched the World Cup.

1 SUBJECT + **2** VERBS
We watched the game and cheered for our team.

2 SUBJECTS + **2** VERBS
My friends and I went to a café and watched the game on their big TV.

Simple Sentence Patterns

Match each sentence with a sentence pattern. Write the letter.

a. 1 SUBJECT + 1 VERB

b. 2 SUBJECTS + 1 VERB

c. 1 SUBJECT + 2 VERBS

d. 2 SUBJECTS + 2 VERBS

_____ **1.** My friends and I play soccer and watch it on TV, too.

_____ **2.** My friends get excited and yell at the TV.

_____ **3.** We all have our favorite players.

_____ **4.** Soccer and basketball are my favorite sports.

Compound Sentences

A **compound sentence** has two subject-verb combinations. To make a compound sentence, connect two simple sentences. Put a comma after the first simple sentence, and then use a coordinating conjunction, such as *and, but,* or *so.*

```
         ┌────────── 1 ──────────┐              ┌── 2 ──┐
My friends  and  I  have  TVs at home, but  we  like  watching games at a café with other fans.
```

PRACTICE 6 Recognizing Compound Sentences

Find four compound sentences in the paragraph. Mark the subjects *S* and the verbs *V*. Circle the comma and the coordinating conjunction.

Once in my life, I spent a whole day shopping. It was in Bangkok at the Chatuchak Weekend Market, the best market in Thailand. It is a huge place, and I was a little worried about getting lost. That day, my friends and I shopped for things for ourselves and our families. I bought some jeans and sandals for myself, and I got silk ties, scarves, and bags as gifts. The prices were good, but I still spent a lot of money. The market also has many places to eat, so we took a lot of breaks for delicious Thai food and cold drinks. We also spent time looking at the exotic birds and fish. It was tiring to spend a whole day shopping, but the time went by fast.

And, *But*, and *So* in Compound Sentences

The coordinating conjunctions *and, but,* and *so* have different meanings.

Rules	Examples
1. Use *and* to add information.	I went shopping, and I bought souvenirs of my trip.
2. Use *but* when the second idea is different or surprising.	I bought a lot of things, but I did not spend a lot of money.
3. Use *so* to show a result.	My family liked their gifts, so I was happy about that.

See Appendix D, page 212, for more information about coordinating conjunctions.

| PRACTICE 7 | Creating Compound Sentences |

Combine each pair of simple sentences into a compound sentence. Use the coordinating conjunction in parentheses.

1. In April of last year, my son was six years old. My daughter was four.

   (and) <u>In April of last year, my son was six years old, and my daughter was four.</u>

2. One day, my children were at home. My friend's little boy was there, too.

   (and) _____

3. The children were in the kitchen. I was not with them.

   (but) _____

(continued on next page)

4. My friend's son picked up the phone. He called 911.

   (and) _____

5. He did not talk to the operator. She saw our address on her computer screen.

   (but) _____

6. She believed that we had an emergency. She sent the police to our house.

   (so) _____

7. There was no emergency. The police officers were angry about the call.

   (so) _____

8. I was upset with the children. I had a serious talk with them.

   (so) _____

9. It was just a child's mistake. I had to pay a $50 fine.

   (but) _____

10. I learned a lesson. The children did, too.

   (and) _____

PRACTICE 8 Coordinating Conjunctions

Circle the correct coordinating conjunction.

1. It was a beautiful place, *(and / but)* I was happy there.

2. Hee Eun did not study for the test, *(but / so)* she got a good grade.

3. I liked the movie, *(and / but)* I did not understand all of it.

4. First, I cleaned the kitchen, *(and / so)* then I cleaned the bathroom.

5. It rained all day, *(but / so)* they did not play baseball.

6. The music was great, *(and / but)* there was free food.

7. Their apartment building is nice, *(but / so)* that part of the city is not.

8. The shoes did not fit right, *(but / so)* I did not buy them.

Using Commas

On page 136, you learned about using commas in compound sentences. Here are four more rules for using commas.

RULES	EXAMPLES
1. Use a comma between the date and the year.	I was born on **March 1, 1991**.
2. Use a comma after a time expression or a time-order word at the beginning of a sentence. (Exception: Do not use a comma after *Then*.)	**Last year**, we took a family vacation. **First**, we decided where to go. **Then** I did some research online.
3. Use a comma between items in a series of words or phrases. (Make sure that the items in a series are the same part of speech.)	**Lucia, Rosa, and I** went to the beach. We **went swimming, read magazines**, and **took long walks**.
4. Do not use a comma when you connect only two words or phrases.	**My parents and friends** came to see me in the hospital. I do not remember **the accident or the ambulance ride**.

PRACTICE 9   Correcting Comma Errors

Find the places where 12 commas are missing. Make corrections. One sentence needs no comma.

1. In August of 2012 we celebrated my parents' 25th wedding anniversary.

2. They were married on August 7 1987.

3. My parents invited all our relatives and everyone came to our house for the day.

4. My grandparents aunts uncles and cousins brought many kinds of food.

5. We ate together at a table in our backyard.

6. There were many delicious main dishes salads and desserts.

7. After that the children played games and the adults sat and talked.

8. In the evening we said our goodbyes and everyone went home.

Take a sheet of paper. Write answers to the questions. Use the words in parentheses. You will need one or more commas in each sentence.

What are three things you do not own? (*or*)

I do not own a motorcycle, a horse, or a boat.

1. What are three foods you like? (*and*)
2. What are three subjects you are interested in studying? (*and*)
3. What are three subjects you are not interested in? (*or*)
4. What are three things you do in the morning? (*In the morning*)
5. What are two things you often do on weekends? (*On weekends*)
6. What is today's date? (Give the month, the day, and the year.)

GRAMMAR

THE SIMPLE PAST

Verbs in the **simple past** describe events that began and ended in the past.

IN THE PRESENT

I **watch** the news on TV every day.

Mr. Lee **is** a grandfather now.

IN THE PAST

I **watched** the news on TV yesterday.

Mr. Lee **was** a child in the 1950s.

The Simple Past of the Verb *Be*

In Chapter 1, you learned that the verb *be* has three present forms: *am, are,* and *is*. In the simple past, the verb *be* has only two forms: *was* and *were*.

SIMPLE PAST OF *BE* IN STATEMENTS							
Singular Subject	**Be**	**(Not)**		**Plural Subject**	**Be**	**(Not)**	
I	was			We			
You	were			You	were	(not)	here last week.
He		(not)	here last week.	They			
She	was						
It							

RULES	EXAMPLES
1. The past of *there is/are* is *there was/were*.	There was a meeting yesterday. There were no cars 200 years ago.
2. A past time expression can go at the beginning or end of a sentence.	I was at home yesterday morning. In 1999, Jack was in Singapore.

See Appendix C3, page 200, for contractions with not.
See page 159 for more information about past time expressions.

PRACTICE 10   *Was/Were* in Statements

Ⓐ Change the sentences to the past. Use *was* or *were*.

1. I am here.

Last Friday, ___I was here___ , too.

2. The train is on time.

Yesterday, _____ , too.

3. You are my partner.

_____ three days ago, too.

4. There are six people in the car.

_____ in the car last night, too.

5. My family is on vacation.

Last August, _____ , too.

Ⓑ Change the sentences to the past. Use *was* or *were* + *not*. (Do not use *never*.)

1. I am never late for class.

___I was not late for class___ this morning.

2. You are never late for class.

_____ yesterday.

3. You and I are never partners.

Last semester, _____ .

(continued on next page)

4. There is never much rain here.

_____ last year.

5. My family is not here.

In 1998, _____ .

TRY IT OUT! Take a sheet of paper. Answer the questions in complete sentences. Use _was_ or _were_.

1. When you were a child, what were your favorite TV shows?
2. How was the weather yesterday?
3. Where were you at 6:00 P.M. yesterday?
4. Where were you five years ago?
5. What color was your first (bicycle/car/pet)?
6. How many students were there in your high school?

The Simple Past: Regular Verbs

All **regular verbs** end in _-ed_ in simple past affirmative statements. The verb is the same for all subjects.

REGULAR VERBS IN THE SIMPLE PAST: AFFIRMATIVE STATEMENTS		
Subject	**Simple Past Verb**	
I	**lived**	in Kiev for 17 years.
She	**studied**	engineering at the university.
He	**stopped**	working at age 68.
They	**arrived**	in this country six months ago.

See Appendix C6, page 207, for spelling rules for regular verbs in the simple past.

REGULAR VERBS IN THE SIMPLE PAST: NEGATIVE STATEMENTS			
Subject	*Did Not*	Base Form of Verb	
I		live	with my family.
She	did not	study	music or art.
He		stop	his volunteer work.
They		arrive	by plane.

PRACTICE 11 Spelling Practice

Write the simple past form of each verb. Check Appendix C6 on page 207 for spelling rules.

1. listen _____listened_____   6. plan _____

2. fix _____   7. carry _____

3. need _____   8. decide _____

4. stay _____   9. worry _____

5. cry _____   10. stop _____

PRACTICE 12 Regular Verbs in Negative Statements

Complete the sentences. Repeat the same verb, but make it negative.
Use the past time expression in parentheses.

1. (last night) I often watch TV at night, but I _did not watch TV last night._

2. (last year) They often visit us, but they _____.

3. (yesterday) She often calls me, but she _____.

4. (last night) It often rains, but it _____.

5. (last month) We often travel, but we _____.

6. (last weekend) He often washes his car on weekends, but

   he _____.

Take a sheet of paper. Write ten true statements using the simple past. Use the verbs from the box. Include both affirmative and negative statements. Include time expressions such as *yesterday, last week/month/year*, or *in 2012*.

clean	fix	play	snow	study	wait
cook	listen	rain	stay	talk	walk

EXAMPLES

I listened to music and studied last night.

It did not rain last weekend.

The Simple Past: Irregular Verbs

Irregular verbs do not end in *-ed* in the simple past. Compare two verbs with the same meaning, the irregular verb *begin* and the regular verb *start*:

VERBS IN THE SIMPLE PAST: AFFIRMATIVE STATEMENTS			
		Simple Past Form	
Regular	The class	start**ed**	on time.
Irregular		began	

Many common verbs are irregular, such as *go (went), have (had), get (got),* and *make (made).* You will need to use irregular verbs, so you will need to memorize their simple past forms. You can find a list of common irregular verbs on page 208.

In negative statements, there is no difference between regular and irregular verbs in the simple past. For both types of verbs, use *did not* + the base form of the verb.

VERBS IN THE SIMPLE PAST: NEGATIVE STATEMENTS				
		Did	*Not*	**Base Form of the Verb**
Regular	The class	did	not	start	late.
Irregular				begin	

A Complete the affirmative statements with the words given.
Use the simple past.

1. I / take / a trip with my family

   In 1998, _I took a trip with my family_____.

2. he / go / to his grandparents' house

   Last summer, _____.

3. my cousins / come / to visit me

   _____ last year.

4. she / make / an important decision

   Two years ago, _____.

5. they / leave / early

   _____ yesterday morning.

6. the children / have / fun

   _____ last weekend.

7. I / get / home at 8:00 P.M.

   _____ yesterday evening.

8. I / buy / a new phone

   Last year, _____.

B Change each statement from affirmative to negative.

1. I took a trip. _I did not take a trip._____

2. I hurt myself. _____

3. I forgot my passport. _____

4. I knew his name. _____

5. I said goodbye. _____

6. I did the right thing. _____

| PRACTICE 14 | Editing for Verb Errors |

Find 11 more errors in verbs in this paragraph. Make corrections.

Last Monday, Harry ~~was have~~ *had* a
terrible day. The day begun badly. He
did no remember to set his alarm, so
he got up late. He did not has time
for breakfast. He boughts coffee on
the way to work and spilled it on his
clothes. At work, he wrote reports all
morning. At noon, his boss came in,
and she was angry. "You did not a good job on this report," she say to
Harry. Harry felt bad about his boss's feedback. He no went out to lunch
with his friends. Instead, he was stayed in his office and work. Finally,
he finished. On the way home, he has a car accident. Poor Harry! At
home, he goed back to bed. He wanted to forget the whole day.

| PRACTICE 15 | Statements with the Simple Past |

Write six sentences about Amanda's life using information from the timeline.
Use verbs in the simple past tense.

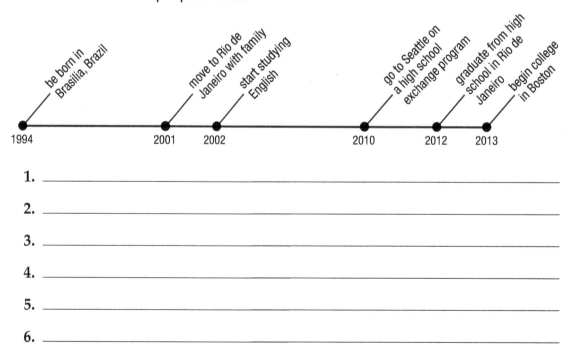

be born in Brasília, Brazil — 1994

move to Rio de Janeiro with family — 2001

start studying English — 2002

go to Seattle on a high school exchange program — 2010

graduate from high school in Rio de Janeiro — 2012

begin college in Boston — 2013

1. _____

2. _____

3. _____

4. _____

5. _____

6. _____

Take a sheet of paper. Write six or more true statements about your life. Use the simple past tense. Try to include both affirmative and negative statements.

I was born in Osaka.

I loved animals, but I did not have a pet.

✎ Applying Vocabulary: Using Adjectives + Prepositions

In this chapter, you have seen many adjectives followed by prepositions. Review the ones you learned about on page 132.

A preposition needs an **object**. That object is usually a noun or an **object pronoun** (*me, you, him, her, it, us, them*).

They were happy **for Maria**. We were happy **for her**, too.

He was nervous **about final exams**. I was nervous **about them**, too.

The object of a preposition can also be a **gerund**. A gerund looks like the *-ing* form of a verb, but a gerund is used as a noun.

	Adjective	Preposition	Gerund	
I was	excited	about	**going**	to college.
	interested	in	**making**	new friends.
	proud	of	**getting**	good grades.

Adjectives + Prepositions

Complete the sentences with the correct preposition.

1. I was happy _____ the result of the game.

2. My friends were happy _____ me when I got the job.

3. I was proud _____ my brother when he became a pilot.

4. Many people are afraid _____ public speaking.

5. We were excited _____ our plans for the weekend.

6. I was always good _____ sports.

7. I was never interested _____ history.

8. Everyone was nervous _____ the test.

Take a sheet of paper. Write five or more true statements, affirmative or negative. Include an adjective + preposition + gerund combination in each statement. Use the verb phrases from the box.

buy a car/house	learn to drive	speak English
get a job	make mistakes	use technology
go away from home	make new friends	

EXAMPLE

I am always interested in making new friends.

WRITING ASSIGNMENT

You are going to write a paragraph about an important event in your life, like the writing models on pages 130 and 131. Before you write, you will have a choice of prewriting activities.

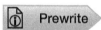 Prewrite

STEP 1: Prewrite to get ideas.

a. Get ready to write by prewriting. Choose one of these activities:

• Make notes in time order about what happened on the day of the event. (See page 133 for an example of notes in time order.)

• Freewrite about the event for at least five minutes. (See page 134 for an explanation of freewriting and an example.)

> **Writing Tip**
>
> Some writers like to do freewriting this way: First, they freewrite for five minutes. Next, they read what they wrote and choose one idea from their writing. Then they freewrite about that idea for five minutes more.

b. Work with a partner. Take turns describing the important event from your life. Then tell your partner three things you remember about the important event in his or her life.

c. Look at your notes or freewriting. Decide what information is most important to your description of the event. Circle or underline it. Decide how you want to organize your paragraph. Use time order or listing order, like the writing models on pages 130 and 131.

STEP 2: Write the first draft.

Write your first draft. Begin with a topic sentence. Make sure your supporting sentences show why your topic sentence is true. Add a title.

STEP 3: Revise and edit the draft.

a. Read your paragraph again. It may help you to read it out loud. Make changes if needed.

b. Do peer review. Sit with a partner and exchange papers. Give each other feedback. Follow the steps on the Peer Review Worksheet.

PEER REVIEW WORKSHEET

Your partner's name: _____

Content

1. Read all of your partner's paragraph.

2. Underline any part of the paragraph you do not understand. Ask your partner to explain it.

3. Circle the topic sentence. If there is no topic sentence, write *TS?* on the paper.

4. Reread the supporting sentences. Ask questions if you want more information.

5. How did your partner organize the paragraph? On the paper, write *Time order* or *Listing order*. If the organization is not clear, write *Order?*.

Format and Language

6. Use this list to check your partner's paper. Check (✓) each item as you finish.

    ☐ the format of the paper   ☐ the use of simple past verbs
    ☐ a subject in every sentence ☐ the use of commas
    ☐ a verb for every subject

7. Put a question mark (?) if you are not sure about something.

---

c. Return your partner's paper. Can you say something nice about it?

d. Look at your own paper. If you do not agree with a comment, ask another student or your teacher.

e. On your paper, mark any changes you want to make to your paragraph.

STEP 4: Write a new draft.

a. Take a new sheet of paper and write a new draft.

b. Edit your new draft carefully, and hand it in to your teacher.

Writing Tip

Contractions are fine for informal writing, but they are not used in academic writing. When you edit a piece of academic writing, such as your paragraph for this assignment, change any contractions to their full forms. For example, change *wasn't* and *didn't* to *was not* and *did not*.

SELF-ASSESSMENT

In this chapter, you learned to:

○ Organize your ideas during prewriting

○ Write compound sentences with *and*, *but*, and *so*

○ Apply rules for using commas in sentences

○ Use simple past verbs

○ Write, revise, and edit a paragraph about an important event in your life

Which ones can you do well? Mark them ☑

Which ones do you need to practice more? Mark them ⊗

EXPANSION

 TIMED WRITING

Students need to write quickly to succeed in academic writing. For example, sometimes students need to do a writing assignment in class or on a test, and they have only a short time to do it.

To practice writing quickly, you are going to write a paragraph in class. You will have 20 minutes. To complete the assignment in time, follow these steps.

1. Read the writing prompt on page 151 (or the prompt that your teacher gives you). Make sure that you understand the prompt. If you have questions, ask your teacher. (2 minutes)

2. Brainstorm to get ideas. On a sheet of paper, make some notes. Then think about organizing your ideas. Mark up your notes with circles, arrows, and numbers to show the order of information in your paragraph. Write a topic sentence for your paragraph. (6 minutes)

3. Write your paragraph. Be sure to include a topic sentence and supporting sentences. (10 minutes)

4. Check your paragraph. Correct any mistakes. (2 minutes)

5. Give your paper to your teacher.

   Prompt: Write about last weekend or some other weekend that you remember well. Choose an adjective to describe the weekend such as *busy, interesting, relaxing, typical, unforgettable,* or *unusual.* Use that adjective in your topic sentence. Describe the events of the weekend so that you support your topic sentence.

 ## YOUR JOURNAL

Continue making entries in your journal. If you cannot think of a topic for a journal entry, try one of these ideas:

- Write about your education. How old were you when you started school? What schools did you go to? How did you feel about school when you were growing up?

- Think of a time when you had some good luck. What happened? Why did you think you were lucky?

- When did you start learning English? Did you choose to study English, or did you have to learn it? Describe your first experiences with learning English.

For more ideas for journal entries, see Appendix A on page 193.

CHAPTER 8

MEMORIES OF A TRIP

OBJECTIVES

Writers need certain skills.

In this chapter, you will learn to:

- End a paragraph with a concluding sentence
- Write past time expressions
- Use *before* and *after* as prepositions
- Write complex sentences with past time clauses
- Identify and correct sentence fragments
- Write, revise, and edit a paragraph about a trip

Going on a trip!

In this chapter, you will be reading about some **memorable** trips. If something is memorable, it is worth remembering. At the end of this chapter, you will write a paragraph about a trip of your own that you remember well.

LOOKING AT THE MODELS

In the writing models, two students share their memories of trips they took.

Work with a partner or in a small group. Read the models. Then answer the questions.

Writing Model 1

A Trip with My Family

I have a happy memory from my childhood. When I was small, my family took a trip to a lake. It was in the summer. We went there early in the morning and stayed all day. I remember playing games on the grass with my brothers and sisters. We climbed trees, too, and that was fun. At noon, my father built a fire, and we made shish kebabs. It was a delicious lunch. After that, I remember lying on a blanket while my older sister told stories. I loved listening to them. I did not want to leave when it was time to go home. I had a lot of fun that day, so I will always remember that trip to the lake.

Questions about the Model

1. **a.** What is the topic of the paragraph? _____

   b. What is the writer's controlling idea about the topic?

   _____

2. What details does the writer give about the trip?

   a. When did it happen? _____

   b. What did the writer do? List three details.

   _____

   _____

   _____

(continued on next page)

3. Did the writer use time order to organize the paragraph? *(Yes / No)*

4. What simple past tense verbs did the writer use in these sentences? Fill in the blanks.

   a. When I _____ small, my family _____ a trip to a lake.

   b. At noon, my father _____ a fire, and we _____ shish kebabs.

   c. I _____ to leave when it _____ time to go home.

✎ Writing Model 2

The Trip That Changed My Life

My trip to the United States was a big shock. One day, my mother said, "Go and pack your clothes. Tomorrow we are going to New York. We are going to live there." The news was a complete surprise to me. I went to my room and sat on the bed for a long time. Then I called my best friend. The next morning, my mother and I got on a plane. I remember sitting next to the window and looking down on my city. I remember feeling scared about my future. After we landed in New York, my aunt picked us up, and we went to stay with her. My life changed overnight. I will never forget that trip.

Questions about the Model

1. a. What is the topic of the paragraph? _____

   b. What is the writer's controlling idea about the topic?

   _____

2. Why was the trip a shock for the writer? Check (✓) your answers.
   - ☐ His mother's plans surprised him.
   - ☐ He had to say goodbye to his mother.
   - ☐ He was afraid to get on an airplane.
   - ☐ Big changes happened in his life very fast.

3. Did the writer use time order to organize the paragraph? *(Yes / No)*

4. What simple past tense verbs did the writer use in these sentences? Fill in the blanks.

    a. One day, my mother _____ , "Go and pack your clothes."

    b. I _____ to my room and _____ on the bed for a long time.

    c. The next morning, my mother and I _____ on a plane.

Looking at Vocabulary: Word Families

When you learn a new word, try to learn the other words in its word family at the same time. That will help you expand your English vocabulary, and, as a writer, you will have more ways to express your ideas.

Study the two word families in this chart:

	NOUN	VERB	ADJECTIVE
1		forget	forgettable unforgettable
2	memory	remember	memorable

PRACTICE 1   **Word Families**

Choose words from the two families in the word family chart to complete the sentences.

1. a. It was the happiest day of my life, and I will never _____ it.

    b. When something is not worth remembering, such as a boring movie, you can describe it as _____ .

    c. The birth of our first child was an _____ experience.

2. a. Taking the test for my driver's license was a _____ experience.

    b. I _____ taking a trip with my family when I was about seven years old.

    c. The first day of school is an important childhood _____ for many people.

The word *memory* has several meanings. Write the letter for the correct definition of *memory* next to each example sentence.

_____ 1. Do you have good memories of vacations during your childhood?

_____ 2. I have a bad memory for names, but I never forget a face.

_____ 3. My mp3 player has enough memory to hold thousands of songs.

a. the ability to remember things, such as people and experiences

b. something that you remember about a person or an experience

c. the amount of space on a computer for storing information

ORGANIZATION

CONCLUDING SENTENCES

Some paragraphs end with a **concluding sentence**. *Concluding* means "finishing" or "completing." A concluding sentence marks the end of the writer's comments on the topic. It usually connects to information in the topic sentence. Below are two ways for a concluding sentence to do that.

- Sometimes a concluding sentence repeats words from the topic sentence, to bring the reader back to the main idea:

TOPIC SENTENCE | When I take a long trip, I prefer to go by train. The seats on trains are very comfortable. They give me enough space for my legs. I like the big windows on trains, too. I enjoy looking out at the views, especially in the country. I also like being free to leave my seat. I can stand up and walk around on a train when I want to.

CONCLUDING SENTENCE | These are just a few of the reasons why I like to travel by train.

- Sometimes the writer ends the paragraph with a personal comment about the topic:

TOPIC SENTENCE | The first—and only—trip by the *Titanic* is a well-known story. The *Titanic* was a British passenger ship that set out from Southampton, England, on April 10, 1912, to travel to New York City. It carried some of the richest people in the world, many of them famous. It also carried over a thousand much poorer people who were hoping to build better lives in North America. On the night of April 15, the *Titanic* hit an iceberg and sank, killing 1,514 people.

CONCLUDING SENTENCE | Every time I think about the story of the *Titanic*, I feel a great wave of sadness. — PERSONAL COMMENT

Underline the topic sentence and the concluding sentence. Circle the words that connect them.

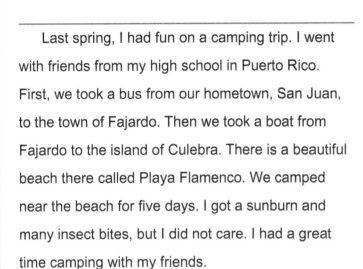

Last spring, I had fun on a camping trip. I went with friends from my high school in Puerto Rico. First, we took a bus from our hometown, San Juan, to the town of Fajardo. Then we took a boat from Fajardo to the island of Culebra. There is a beautiful beach there called Playa Flamenco. We camped near the beach for five days. I got a sunburn and many insect bites, but I did not care. I had a great time camping with my friends.

PRACTICE 4   Choosing a Concluding Sentence

Read each paragraph. Then choose the best concluding sentence. Write that sentence on the lines.

PARAGRAPH 1

The Gift

Last year, during spring break, my parents gave me the gift of a trip. They bought me a plane ticket to visit my brother in Chicago. He and his wife had a new baby boy, and I wanted to see my nephew. I stayed in Chicago for five days and helped take care of the baby. I also did some of the laundry and cooking. I especially remember making the beef stew that my brother loves. _____

_____

a. Now it is a year later, and my little nephew is learning to walk.

b. I tried to help my brother and sister-in-law as much as possible.

c. That trip was a gift from my parents to me and from me to my brother.

(continued on next page)

PARAGRAPH 2

A Wonderful City

I love Florence, Italy, for three reasons. First of all, I enjoy the people of Florence. They are friendly, interesting, and good-looking. Second, I like to hear people speak Italian. I think it is a beautiful language. Finally, I love the food in Florence. You can get delicious things to eat in the markets, shops, and restaurants. _____

_____

a. Millions of people visit Florence because it is a historic city.

b. The people, language, and food make Florence one of my favorite places.

c. It is also interesting to learn about the art and architecture of this beautiful city.

PARAGRAPH 3

The Secrets to a Successful Restaurant

There are four keys to running a successful restaurant. First, the food must taste good. Boring or bad food will not bring in customers. Second, the dining room must be a comfortable and attractive place. People should feel good spending time in the restaurant. Third, there must be good service. Both the kitchen staff and the servers need to do their jobs well. Finally, the price must be right. There must be a good match between the cost and the dining experience. _____

_____

a. The restaurant should stay open late, too.

b. A restaurant that does well in these four areas will be a success.

c. Many new restaurants fail and have to close after just a few months.

PARAGRAPH 4

The Power of Television

Television has a big influence on children today. In some countries, children spend a lot of time watching it. For example, in the United States, the average child watches television three or four hours a day. Many children spend more time each year in front of a TV than in school. _____

a. Personally, I worry about the influence of television on my own children.

b. In fact, almost all American homes today have one or more TV sets.

c. The Internet also has a very big influence on many children today.

GRAMMAR

PAST TIME EXPRESSIONS

A **past time expression** tells when something happened. It often comes at the beginning or end of a sentence. When it is at the beginning of a sentence, put a comma after it.

I was absent from class **the day before yesterday**.

The day before yesterday, I was absent from class.

Past Time Expressions with *Ago* or *Last*

The words *ago* and *last* are used in some past time expressions.

RULES	EXAMPLES
1. Use an amount of time + *ago*.	It happened **many years** ago. They left **five minutes** ago.
2. Use *last* + a period of time.	It happened last **summer**. They left last **week**.

Using *Ago* or *Last*

Fill in the blanks with *ago* or *last* to complete the paragraph.

_____Last_____ year, Raquel took several business trips. In
     1.

January, she was in South Africa for ten days. Then she went to Brazil

_____ March. It was not her first trip to South America.
        2.

She was also there in 2000 and again four years _____. Her
                                                        3.

next trip was _____ May, to Hong Kong. She has been there
                    4.

several times, too. In fact, she was there a week _____. Then
                                                          5.

_____ fall, Raquel went on two trips to Europe. Many years
        6.

_____, when she was a little girl, she dreamed about seeing
        7.

the world. Now her dream has come true.

Prepositional Phrases for Describing Past Time

The prepositions *in, on,* and *for* are used in some past time expressions.

RULES	EXAMPLES
1. Use *in* + a month, season, or year.	It happened in **July**.
	It happened in **1922**.
2. Use *on* + a specific day or date.	It happened on **July 1**, 1922.
	The baby was born on **Friday**.
3. Use *for* + an amount of time.	We waited for **15 minutes**.

In, *On*, and *For* in Past Time Expressions

Fill in the blanks with *in*, *on*, or *for* to complete the statements.

1. He graduated _____ 2006.

2. I was born _____ March 13, 1987.

3. We stayed there _____ ten days.

4. I bought my ticket _____ Monday.

5. She went on vacation _____ April.

6. They were away _____ a week.

7. Their trip began _____ August 8.

8. We waited _____ an hour.

9. We got married _____ the spring.

10. The wedding was _____ May 1, 2001.

TRY IT OUT! Take a sheet of paper. Write ten true statements about your life. Use the past time expressions in the list.

_____ days ago   *I went to the zoo four days ago.*

1. last weekend

2. last summer

3. one year ago

4. in 1999

5. in 2012

6. for a long time

7. for _____ years

8. _____ days ago

9. _____ years ago

10. on _____

Before and *After* as Prepositions

Before and *after* are sometimes used as prepositions. A prepositional phrase with *before* or *after* describes time. Use a noun or a gerund as the object of the preposition.

PREPOSITION + NOUN
I was nervous **before** the **flight**.

PREPOSITION + GERUND
I was nervous **before getting** on the plane.

RULES	EXAMPLES
1. Use *after* + an earlier event.	They took a trip after getting married. (first, the wedding; then the trip)
2. Do not use *after* without an object.	They got married and took a trip after.
3. Use *before* + a later event.	I talked to the teacher before class. (first, the talk; then the class)
4. Put the prepositional phrase at the beginning or end of a sentence. The meaning is the same.	Before class, I talked to the teacher. (first, the talk; then the class)

PRACTICE 7   Combining Sentences with *After* and *Before*

Take a sheet of paper. Combine the two sentences, keeping the time and word order the same. Use *after* or *before* + the boldfaced words.

After
~~We finished~~ **work**. We went fishing.
After work, we went fishing.

before
I washed my hands. ~~I had~~ **lunch**.
I washed my hands before lunch.

1. I studied. I took **the test**.

2. He had **an interview**. He got the job.

3. I spent **a day at the beach**. I had a sunburn.

4. I sent out invitations. I had **my birthday party**.

5. We went on **our vacation**. We told our friends about it.

6. He read the newspaper. He went to **work**.

Take a sheet of paper. Write four true statements with *before* and four true statements with *after*. Use the nouns and gerunds from the box, or choose other objects.

I was nervous before taking my final exams.
I had coffee after my first class.

breakfast	class	graduating from _____
lunch	exam	getting married
dinner	doing homework	having a baby

SENTENCE STRUCTURE

SENTENCES WITH PAST TIME CLAUSES

Past Time Clauses and Independent Clauses

A **past time clause** tells when something happened.

PAST TIME CLAUSE
They saw the Taj Mahal when they were in India.

A past time clause must have three things:
  (1) a time word
  (2) a subject
  (3) a verb

              (1)   (2) (3)
We said goodbye before we left.

A past time clause cannot be a complete sentence by itself. It must connect to an **independent clause.** An independent clause can be a complete sentence.

I went to Buenos Aires. =
{
an independent clause

a complete sentence
}

INDEPENDENT CLAUSE   PAST TIME CLAUSE
I went to Buenos Aires after I finished school.

Sentences with time clauses are **complex sentences.**

See Appendix D, page 213, for more information about complex sentences.

Identifying Clauses

Look at each group of words. Check (✓) *Independent Clause* or *Past Time Clause*.

	INDEPENDENT CLAUSE	PAST TIME CLAUSE
1. when Mei Li and I heard about the concert	☐	☑
2. we decided to buy tickets	☑	☐
3. we stood in line for an hour before the concert	☐	☐
4. a lot of our friends came	☐	☐
5. before the concert started	☐	☐
6. the concert lasted more than three hours	☐	☐
7. the band played some of their greatest hits	☐	☐
8. after they played some of their new music	☐	☐
9. when the concert ended	☐	☐
10. Mei Li and I went out to eat	☐	☐

Past Time Clauses with *Before*, *After*, and *When*

Before, *after*, and *when* are **subordinating conjunctions** in time clauses.

RULES	EXAMPLES
1. Use *after* + something that happened earlier.	THIS HAPPENED **FIRST.** He went to bed **after** he brushed his teeth.
2. Use *before* + something that happened later.	THIS HAPPENED **LATER.** He brushed his teeth **before** he went to bed.
3. Use *when* + something that happened at the same time or soon afterward.	THIS HAPPENED **AT THE SAME TIME.** Everybody cried **when** we said goodbye.
4. A past time clause can come before or after the independent clause. Put a comma after the time clause when it comes first.	**When we said goodbye,** everybody cried.

Complex Sentences with *Before* and *After*

Work alone or with a partner. Write *1* above the action that happened first and *2* above the action that happened later. Underline the past time clause in each sentence.

                2   1

1. Mariela and Ricardo met <u>after they entered the London School of Economics</u>.

2. Mariela knew Ricardo's friends before she met him.

3. After Ricardo heard about Mariela, he wanted to meet her.

4. He fell in love soon after he met her.

5. Before Mariela agreed to marry Ricardo, he had to meet her family in Venezuela.

6. Ricardo and Mariela graduated from the university before they got married.

7. They went on a honeymoon after they got married.

8. After they returned from their trip, they found jobs in Caracas.

TRY IT OUT! Take a sheet of paper. Write sentences with past time clauses to answer the questions. Use *after*, *before*, or *when*. Underline each past time clause.

> When did you start school?
> *I started school <u>when I was five years old</u>.*

> When did you buy a ticket before you did something?
> *I bought a ticket <u>before I took a train</u> last weekend.*

1. Did your parents decide on your name before or after you were born?
2. When did you start learning English?
3. Did you get this book before or after you went to the first class?
4. When did you buy new clothes before you did something?
5. When did you feel nervous before you did something?
6. When did you feel good after you did something?
7. When did you make an important decision?
8. When did you have fun with a friend?

SENTENCE FRAGMENTS

A fragment is a broken piece of something. A **sentence fragment** is a piece of a sentence, not a complete sentence. Something is missing. A past time clause by itself is a sentence fragment.

FRAGMENT   COMPLETE SENTENCE (INDEPENDENT CLAUSE)
After I checked my bag. **I went through airport security.**

Here are two ways to correct a fragment like *After I checked my bag.*

- Connect the fragment to a complete sentence.

PAST TIME CLAUSE   +   INDEPENDENT CLAUSE
After I checked my bag, **I went through airport security.**

- Change the fragment to make it a complete sentence.

First, I checked my bag.

PRACTICE 10	Editing for Sentence Fragments

Read the paragraph. Find four more sentence fragments. Make corrections. Add commas as needed.

Yesterday, Vincent went ~~shopping. After~~ *shopping after* he finished his classes. He needed new running shoes because his old shoes were worn out. After he arrived at the store. He started trying on shoes. Some shoes did not feel right, and some were too expensive. He tried on several pairs of shoes. Before he found the right ones. When he went to pay for them. He realized that he did not have his wallet. It was not in his pocket. He asked the salesperson to hold the shoes for him. He needed to come back later. After he found his wallet in his room. He went back and got his new shoes.

Applying Vocabulary: Using Word Families

When you write your paragraph about a trip, you will probably want to use words from the word family chart you studied on page 155. Here are some tips for using those words.

Memory

When you use the noun *memory* to refer to something you remember, you can use the singular or plural form.

> I have a vivid **memory** of that trip.

> That song brings back fond **memories** of the summer of 2004.

Remember, Forget

After the verb *remember* or *forget,* you can use:

- a noun

  I remember my first **trip** to the ocean.

  I will never forget that **experience**.

- an object pronoun

  I remember **him** clearly.

  I will never forget **her**.

- a gerund

  I remember **seeing** the city lights from the plane.

  I will never forget **saying** goodbye to my friends.

PRACTICE 11 Words after *Remember/Forget*

Look at the writing models on pages 153 and 154. Underline the five uses of *remember* and the one use of *forget*. Find the word used after each verb and circle it.

PRACTICE 12 Using Forms of *Remember, Forget,* and *Memory*

Complete the sentences with true information.

1. I have happy memories from when I was _____ years old. For

   example, I remember _____.

2. I had an unforgettable experience when I was _____ years old.

   I remember _____.

3. I will never forget _____.

4. When I hear the song _____, it brings back memories

   of _____.

You are going to write a paragraph about a trip you took, like the writing models on pages 153 and 154. You will have a choice of prewriting activities.

 Prewrite

STEP 1: Prewrite to get ideas.

a. Get ready to write by doing a prewriting activity. Choose one of these activities:

- Make notes about the trip in time order. (See page 133 for an example of notes in time order.)
- Freewrite about the trip for at least five minutes. (See page 134 for an explanation of freewriting and an example.)

Writing Tip

When you prepare to write a paragraph, think about your readers. What will they want to know about your topic? Working with a partner during the writing process helps you understand the needs of your readers.

b. Find a partner and take turns asking about each other's trips. Ask questions like these:

- Where did you go on your trip?
- When did you go?
- Who went with you?
- How long was your trip?
- What did you do on your trip?
- How did you feel about the trip?
- What do you remember most about your trip?

c. Look again at your notes or freewriting. Add information as needed. Include answers to the questions above. Underline the information that will be most important to describe your trip.

Write

STEP 2: Write the first draft.

Write your first draft. Begin your paragraph with a topic sentence. See the writing models on pages 153 and 154 for examples. Give details in your supporting sentences. Try to include both past time expressions and past time clauses. End your paragraph with a concluding sentence.

Edit

STEP 3: Revise and edit the draft.

a. Read your paragraph again. It may help you to read it out loud. Make changes if needed.

b. Do peer review. Sit with a partner and exchange papers. Give each other feedback. Follow the steps on the Peer Review Worksheet.

PEER REVIEW WORKSHEET

Your partner's name: _____

Content

1. Read all of your partner's paragraph.

2. Underline any part of the paragraph you do not understand. Ask your partner to explain it.

3. Circle the topic sentence. If there is no topic sentence, write *TS?* on the paper.

4. Reread the supporting sentences. Ask questions if you want more information, or if it is not clear when the events happened.

5. Circle the concluding sentence. If there is no concluding sentence, write *CS?* on the paper.

Format and Language

6. Use this list to check your partner's paragraph. Check (✓) each item in the list as you finish.

   ☐ a subject in every sentence   ☐ the use of *before* and *after*
   ☐ a verb for every subject   ☐ the use of commas
   ☐ the use of past tense verbs

7. Put a question mark (?) if you are not sure about something.

---

c. Return your partner's paper. Can you say something nice about it?

d. Look at your own paper. If you do not agree with the feedback on it, ask another student or your teacher. Mark any changes you want to make.

 Write

STEP 4: Write a new draft.

Writing Tip
Experienced writers know that good writing comes from re-writing. Do more than one draft and edit carefully.

a. Take a new sheet of paper and write a new draft.

b. Edit your new draft carefully. Then hand it in to your teacher.

EXPANSION

 ## TIMED WRITING

Students need to write quickly to succeed in academic writing. For example, sometimes students need to do a writing assignment in class or on a test, and they have only a short time to do it.

To practice writing quickly, you are going to write a paragraph in class. You will have 20 minutes. To complete the assignment in time, follow these steps.

1. Read the writing prompt below (or the prompt that your teacher gives you). Make sure that you understand the prompt. If you have questions, ask your teacher. (2 minutes)

2. Brainstorm to get ideas. On a piece of paper, make some notes. Then think about organizing your ideas. Mark up your notes with circles, arrows, and numbers to show the order of information in your paragraph. Write a topic sentence for your paragraph. (6 minutes)

3. Write your paragraph. Be sure to include a topic sentence, supporting sentences, and a concluding sentence. (10 minutes)

4. Check your paragraph. Correct any mistakes. (2 minutes)

5. Give your paper to your teacher.

   Prompt: Write a paragraph about an experience you remember from when you were a child.

YOUR JOURNAL

Continue making entries in your journal. If you cannot think of a topic for a journal entry, try one of these ideas:

- Write about your memories of another trip you took. Tell where and when you made this trip. Focus on describing one thing that you heard, smelled, saw, or tasted on this trip.

- Describe a time when someone or something surprised you. What happened? Was it a good surprise or a bad surprise? Why?

- Write about one of your earliest memories of English. Did you hear a song in English? Did you learn a word in English? What made this experience memorable?

For more ideas for journal entries, see Appendix A on page 193.

CHAPTER 9

LOOKING AHEAD

What is he looking forward to?

In this chapter, you will be reading about people's plans for the future, both the near future (a time that is coming soon) and the distant future (a time that may be years away). You will also write a paragraph about your own plans.

LOOKING AT THE MODELS

In the writing models, two students share their plans and hopes for the future.

Work with a partner or in a small group. Read the models. Then answer the questions.

✎ **Writing Model 1**

My Vacation

I am going to go home for two weeks during winter break, and I am looking forward to spending time with my family and friends. First of all, it will be great to relax with my family. Everyone will be glad to see me, especially my little brothers. I am looking forward to eating my mother's cooking, too. I will also enjoy spending time with my friends. Maybe there will be some parties to go to. We will definitely return to our favorite cafés to eat and listen to music. Most of all, I am looking forward to talking with my friends face to face. We will have a lot to talk about after all this time. I cannot wait to be back home!

Questions about the Model

1. What is the topic of this paragraph? _____

2. What does "I am looking forward to (something)" mean? Circle *a* or *b*.

   a. I am nervous about something in the future.

   b. I am happy about something in the future.

3. What does "I cannot wait to (do something)" mean? Circle *a* or *b*.

   a. I am not able to wait, so I must do it now.

   b. I am very excited that I am going to do it.

4. How does the writer organize his paragraph? Circle: *(Time order / Listing order)*

(continued on next page)

5. What verbs does the writer use to describe future events? Fill in the blanks.

   a. I _____ home for two weeks during winter break, . . .

   b. First of all, it _____ great to relax with my family.

✎ Writing Model 2

` '  X  ' ' ' I ' I ' I ' 1 ' ' ' I ' I ' 2 ' ' ' I ' I ' 3 ' ' ' I ' I ' 4 ' ' ' I ' I ' 5 ' ' ' I ' I ' 6  △ ' '`

My Future

I have big plans for my future. After I learn more English, I am going to study nursing. I am going to apply to a university, perhaps in Texas or California, when I finish the English program here. At the university, I plan to get a bachelor's degree. Then I am probably going to work in a hospital. I hope that I will find a good job as a nurse. I also hope to get married someday. I would like to meet a kind and intelligent man. I would like to have four children, two boys and two girls. I am looking forward to my career, but my family will definitely be the most important part of my future.

Questions about the Model

1. What is the topic sentence? Circle the topic and underline the controlling idea.

2. In what order does the writer expect to reach these goals? Number them from *1* to *6*.

   _____ have children

   ___1___ learn more English

   _____ study nursing

   _____ get a job in a hospital

   _____ get a bachelor's degree

   _____ apply to a university

3. What word means "at some time far in the future"? _____

4. What word means "years of work in a professional job"? _____

5. How did the writer use **future time clauses**? Complete the sentences.

   a. _____ , I am going to study nursing.

   b. I am going to apply to a university, perhaps in Texas or California,

   _____ .

6. What tense is the verb you wrote in each future time clause above? Circle:
   (simple present / future)

Looking at Vocabulary: Adverbs of Probability

Adverbs are a very common part of speech. They have many uses:

- Some adverbs express time, such as *now, soon,* and *then.*
- Some adverbs tell how often an action happens, such as *always, sometimes,* and *never.*
- Some adverbs describe how someone does something, such as *fast, quietly,* or *easily.*

The words *maybe, perhaps, probably,* and *definitely* are also adverbs. They are sometimes called **adverbs of probability**. In the writing models, the writers used these adverbs when writing about future plans and events. These adverbs tell something about the writer's thinking. They tell how sure the writer is that something will happen.

> **PRACTICE 1**   Adverbs of Probability

Ⓐ Find and circle the adverbs *maybe, perhaps, probably,* and *definitely* in the writing models. Underline the sentences.

Ⓑ Why did the writers use *maybe, perhaps, probably,* and *definitely* in those sentences? Write the adverbs to complete the statements.

   1. _____ means that the writer is very sure that something will happen.

   2. _____ means that the writer is almost sure that something will happen.

   3. _____ and _____ both mean that the writer is not sure if something will happen.

LISTING ORDER

One way to organize a paragraph about the future is to use listing order. Writers can use listing order if they do not know the time order of future events or if the order in time is not important.

The author of Writing Model 1 on page 173 used listing order. He organized the information about his vacation plans into two areas: time with his family and time with his friends.

> I am going to go home for two weeks during winter break, and I am looking forward to spending time with my family and friends. First of all, it will be great to relax with my family. Everyone will be glad to see me, especially my little brothers. I am looking forward to eating my mother's cooking, too. I will also enjoy spending time with my friends. Maybe there will be some parties to go to. We will definitely return to our favorite cafés to eat and listen to music. Most of all, I am looking forward to talking with my friends face to face. We will have a lot to talk about after all this time. I cannot wait to be back home!

First of all, also, and *most of all* are **listing-order words**. They help the reader see the organization of the writer's ideas. Notice the position of *also* in *I will also enjoy spending time with my friends. Also* comes before the main verb. The other listing-order words go at the beginning of the sentence.

Here are more listing-order words and phrases:

First	**In addition**	**Second**	**Third**	**Finally**

For more examples of paragraphs with listing order, see:
- "My Wedding Day" on page 131
- "A Wonderful City" on page 158
- "The Secrets to a Successful Restaurant" on page 158

When you read these paragraphs, notice the topic sentences and the listing-order words and phrases.

Topic Sentences for Listing-Order Paragraphs

Work alone or with a partner. Check (✓) the topic sentences that tell the reader that the paragraph will be in listing order.

☑ **1.** There are several reasons I want to be a lawyer.

☐ **2.** There are different kinds of engineers.

☐ **3.** Becoming a doctor will take me a long time.

☐ **4.** A good nurse needs to have four important qualities.

☐ **5.** My grandfather had an important career in public service.

☐ **6.** I have two main reasons for wanting to be a teacher.

☐ **7.** My mother changed careers at age 40.

☐ **8.** The Career Development Office can help students in many ways.

Listing-Order Words

Use four words or phrases from the box to fill in the blanks. For some, there may be more than one possible answer. Add capital letters and commas as needed.

also	finally	first	first of all
in addition	most of all	second	third

---

www.myblog.com

My wife and I are celebrating—we just found a house we want to buy! We need to move for several reasons. _____ (1.), we now live in a small apartment, but we are going to have a baby, so we need more space. _____ (2.), our apartment is on the third floor, and there is no elevator. Three flights of stairs are difficult with

a baby. _____ (3.),
I don't like parking my car on the street,
and our new house will have a garage.

_____ (4.), we are
going to need a guest room because my
mother-in-law is coming to stay with us after
the baby is born. I hope we can get the house
and move in soon because we do not have
much time!

EXPRESSING FUTURE TIME WITH *BE GOING TO*

Verbs with *be going to* express future time.

Statements with *Be Going To*

SINGULAR				
Subject	*Be*	*(Not)*	*Going To*	**Base Form of Main Verb**
I	am			
You	are			
He		(not)	going to	win.
She	is			
It				

PLURAL				
Subject	*Be*	*(Not)*	*Going To*	**Base Form of Main Verb**
We				
You	are	(not)	going to	win.
They				

See Appendix C3, page 199, for the contracted forms of am, is, *and* are (+ not).

RULES	EXAMPLES
1. Use *be going to* for future plans (to tell what someone has already decided to do).	I am going to be at home **in June**. We are going to invite all our friends to the party.
2. Use *be going to* for predictions or guesses about the future.	**I think** the weather is going to be nice. You are going to love this song.
3. Use *and* or *or* to add a second main verb. Do not repeat *be going to*.	She is going to call and **give** us the news. I am not going to call or **write** to him.

Statements with *Be Going To*

Complete each sentence with the correct form of *be going to*. Use the verb in parentheses.

1. (have) I _am going to have_ a day off next Monday.

2. (not, go) I _____ to work that day.

3. (not, work) Next Monday is a holiday, so most people

   _____ .

4. (be) I think the weather _____ great.

5. (go) My friends and I _____ to a lake.

6. (be) I think there _____ seven of us.

7. (take) We _____ the bus.

8. (not, cost) It _____ much.

9. (be) I think it _____ fun.

10. (come) I hope that you _____ , too!

Writing Tip

You can use *I think* or *I do not think* to introduce a statement when you are not sure about a plan or a prediction:

I think I am going to take an economics class.

I do not think I am going to take any history classes.

TRY IT OUT! Take a sheet of paper. Answer the questions. Write complete sentences with *be going to*. Use *I think / I do not think* if you are not sure about what is going to happen.

1. What are you going to do this evening?

2. What time are you going to get up tomorrow?

3. What do you think the weather is going to be like tomorrow?

4. Who do you think is going to call you soon?

5. Where are you going to be next summer?

6. What is something important that you are going to do in your future?

EXPRESSING FUTURE TIME WITH *WILL*

Verbs with *will* also express future time.

Statements with *Will*

SINGULAR				
Subject	***Will***	***(Not)***	**Base Form of Main Verb**	
I				
You			be	on time.
He	will	(not)		
She			need	help.
It				

PLURAL				
Subject	***Will***	***(Not)***	**Base Form of Main Verb**	
We			be	on time.
You	will	(not)		
They			need	help.

See Appendix C8, page 210, for contractions.

RULES	EXAMPLES
1. Use *will* for predictions about the future. In this case, *will* and *be going to* have the same meaning.	You **will love** this song. = You are going to love this song.
2. Use *be going to*, usually not *will*, to announce plans you have already made.	Chris and I **are going to get** married.
3. Use *and* or *or* to add a second main verb. Do not repeat *will*.	She **will go** and **ask**. He probably **will not call** or **write**.

Predictions with *Will*

Use *will* to rewrite these predictions. The meaning of the sentences does not change.

1. I think you are going to enjoy your trip to the islands.

   I think you will enjoy your trip to the islands.

2. The weather is going to be great.

   _____

3. You are not going to need any warm clothes.

   _____

4. The surfing is going to be excellent.

   _____

5. The beaches are not going to be crowded.

   _____

6. We are going to miss you.

   _____

Correcting Verb Errors

Find the verb error in each statement about the future. Make corrections. For some, there may be more than one possible correction.

   will be or *is going to be*
1. Dinner ~~will to be~~ ready soon.

2. I think it's will be sunny tomorrow.

3. I think both of my brothers going to study chemistry.

4. Your adviser will going to help you.

5. I think Brazil will winning the next World Cup.

6. Hiral is going have her baby in May.

7. The party going to start at 9:00 P.M.

8. Juan Carlos will goes to work at 3:00 P.M.

9. I think the next bus will coming soon.

10. Thanks, but I don't think I'm will need a ride tomorrow.

FUTURE TIME EXPRESSIONS

Future time expressions tell when events will happen. They can help show the time and order of events in a paragraph.

Using *This*, *Next*, or *In*

The words *this*, *next*, and *in* are used in some future time expressions.

RULES	EXAMPLES
1. Use *this* + a specific time period. The time period is happening now (as in *this year*) or will begin soon (as in *this weekend*).	They will finish the job this **week**. I am going to leave this **evening**.
2. Use *next* + a specific time period. The time period will begin in the future.	We will not be here next **week**. He is going to graduate next **year**.
3. Use *in* + an amount of time (such as a number of hours, days, or years). The event will happen after that time passes.	She is going to be back in **a minute**. In **two weeks**, it will be spring.

PRACTICE 7   Using *This*, *Next*, or *In*

Circle the correct word to complete the statements.

1. Jack is going to graduate *(in / this)* two years.

2. This summer, I am going to take classes, but *(this / next)* summer, I am going to work.

3. Rima is probably studying right now because she is going to have an exam *(in / this)* afternoon.

4. The students are on spring break now, so there are no classes *(this / next)* week.

5. Professor: Your paper is due on Tuesday.

   Student: Do you mean tomorrow?

   Professor: No, not this week. *(Next / In)* Tuesday.

6. The semester began three weeks ago. It will end *(next / in)* 12 weeks.

Take a sheet of paper. Answer the questions. Write complete sentences and include the time expressions.

1. What are you going to do tomorrow?
2. Where are you going to be the day after tomorrow?
3. What are you going to do this weekend?
4. Where are you going to be next week?
5. What is going to happen in a few years?

SENTENCE STRUCTURE

SENTENCES WITH FUTURE TIME CLAUSES

Future Time Clauses and Independent Clauses

A **future time clause** tells when something will happen.

FUTURE TIME CLAUSE

He is going to travel after he graduates.

Like a past time clause, a future time clause needs three things:

(1) a time word
(2) a subject
(3) a verb

(1) (2) (3)

I will call you when I arrive.

A future time clause is never a complete sentence by itself. It must connect to an independent clause. An independent clause is different from a time clause; it can be a complete sentence.

She is going to get a job. = { an independent clause / a complete sentence }

After she graduates. = a sentence fragment (not a complete sentence)

INDEPENDENT CLAUSE   + FUTURE TIME CLAUSE

She is going to get a job after she graduates.

Sentences with time clauses are called **complex sentences**, and the time words in these sentences are called **subordinating conjunctions**.

See Appendix D, page 213, for more information about complex sentences.

Check (✓) the sentences with future time clauses. Underline the future time clause.

☐ **1.** Vote for me next election day!

☑ **2.** <u>When I become president</u>, I will work for world peace.

☐ **3.** Together, we are going to put an end to all wars.

☐ **4.** I am also going to make education a high priority.

☐ **5.** After I am president, there will be more money for our children's schools.

☐ **6.** I am going to make sure we have clean air and clean water.

☐ **7.** I will stop polluters before they destroy our environment.

☐ **8.** I am going to do great things after I win this election!

Future Time Clauses with *Before*, *After*, and *When*

The words *before, after,* and *when* can introduce future time clauses.

RULES	EXAMPLES
1. Use a simple present verb in a future time clause. Do not use *will* or *be going to*.	He will ask his advisor when he sees her. We are going to review before class ends today.
2. A future time clause can come before or after the independent clause. The meaning is the same.	I am going to go to medical school after I finish college. After I finish college, I am going to go to medical school.
3. Do not use *after* alone. Use it in a prepositional phrase or to introduce a time clause.	I am going to graduate and get a job after that. OR After I graduate, I am going to get a job. NOT: I am going to graduate and get a job ~~after~~.

PRACTICE 9 Verbs in Sentences with Future Time Clauses

Circle the correct verb. Underline the independent clause in each sentence once and underline the future time clause twice.

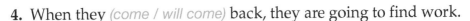

1. Sonia and Tony are going to get married after they *(finish / will finish)* school.

2. I *(am / will be)* there when they have their wedding in June.

3. After they *(are / are going to be)* married, they are going to take a trip.

4. When they *(come / will come)* back, they are going to find work.

5. They *(look / will look)* for a place to live after they have jobs.

6. They are probably going to wait before they *(have / will have)* children.

7. Before they start a family, they *(buy / are going to buy)* a house.

8. I hope they will be very happy when they *(are / will be)* married.

PRACTICE 10 Using *After*

Look at Omar's schedule for Friday. Take a sheet of paper and write four sentences with *after* about things he is going to do. Use both *after* + noun and *after* + subject and verb. Underline each phrase or clause with *after*.

> After coffee with Luisa, Omar is going to go to his math class.
>
> He's going to return a library book after his math test is over.

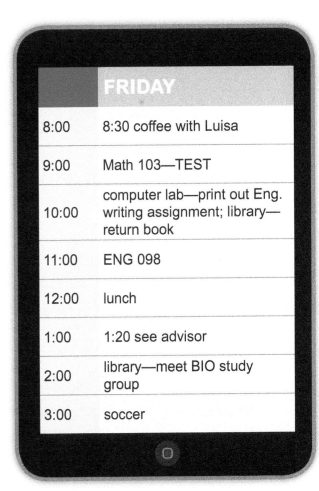

FRIDAY	
8:00	8:30 coffee with Luisa
9:00	Math 103—TEST
10:00	computer lab—print out Eng. writing assignment; library—return book
11:00	ENG 098
12:00	lunch
1:00	1:20 see advisor
2:00	library—meet BIO study group
3:00	soccer

TRY IT OUT! Take a sheet of paper. Complete the sentences with an independent clause or a future time clause. Use your own ideas.

After I finish this exercise, *I will give my paper to the teacher.*

1. After I finish this exercise, . . .
2. Before I go to bed tonight, . . .
3. . . . after I get up tomorrow.
4. I am going to have something to eat . . .
5. . . . , I am going to relax.
6. . . . , I will be happy.

RUN-ON SENTENCES

A **run-on sentence** is a mistake. Run-on sentences happen when writers do not connect independent clauses correctly. In the list, there are examples of several types of run-on sentences. You will see one way to correct each one.

THERE IS NO
CONNECTING WORD.

1. **Run-On:** I am interested in police work my major is criminology.

   What to do: Add a comma + a coordinating conjunction (such as *and*, *but*, or *so*).

   Correct: I am interested in police work, and my major is criminology.

A COMMA CANNOT
CONNECT TWO SENTENCES.

2. **Run-On:** I am going to study math, I am going to become an engineer.

   What to do: Revise the sentence to connect the two verbs with *and*.

   Correct: I am going to study math and become an engineer.

THEN IS NOT A
CONNECTING WORD.

3. **Run-On:** They are going to save their money, then they will buy a house.

   What to do: Revise as two simple sentences.

   Correct: They are going to save their money. Then they will buy a house.

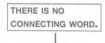
A COMMA CANNOT
CONNECT TWO SENTENCES.

4. **Run-On:** I left him a message, he called me back.

   What to do: Use a subordinating conjunction such as *because*, *after*, *when*, or *before*.

   Correct: After I left him a message, he called me back.

Identifying Run-On Sentences

Work alone or with a partner. Write *RO* next to each run-on sentence. Write *OK* next to each correct sentence.

OK   **1.** In the year 2030, I think my life will be very different.

RO   **2.** I will be much older I will be middle-aged.

_____ **3.** I am not married now, in 2030 I think I will be married.

_____ **4.** I hope to get married in a few years, after, I hope we will have children.

_____ **5.** Now I do not own a house, but I hope to have a nice one in 2030.

_____ **6.** I am going to finish my education, then I will begin my career.

_____ **7.** After I begin my career, I am going to work very hard.

_____ **8.** I will have a good job in 2030, so my family will be able to live well.

Correcting Run-On Sentences

Find the errors in these run-on sentences. Make corrections. There is more than one way to correct each sentence.

     When we
1. ~~We~~ said goodbye to our friends, I felt sad about leaving my homeland.

2. We began our trip it was very cold.

3. We arrived at the airport, then we went to the ticket counter and checked our bags.

4. This was my first time on a plane it felt like a bus at first.

5. The plane left the ground, it made my stomach feel strange.

6. We flew for a few hours, then we landed in Canada.

7. We walked off the plane my relatives were there.

8. I missed my friends, I was excited about starting a new life.

PRACTICE 13   Editing for Run-On Sentences

Find six more run-on sentences in this paragraph. Make corrections. There is more than one way to correct each run-on.

Q www.myblog.com

1 Someday, I am going to take a trip around the world. 2 I plan to spend six months
                    and
on my trip, I expect to travel mostly by plane.
                    ^
3 My first stop will be in Hawaii I want to try surfing and visit a volcano. 4 From Hawaii, I am going to fly to Japan, I also want to visit

Pyramids in Egypt

Korea, China, Thailand, and Indonesia. 5 In each country, I am going to spend some time in the countryside and some in the city, I especially want to see Kyoto and Beijing. 6 After two months in Asia, I am going to fly to eastern Africa. 7 I want to go on a photo safari to see wild animals, of course, I will have my camera. 8 My next flight will take me north to Egypt, so I can see the pyramids, after that, I am going to travel to Istanbul. 9 I look forward to spending the last part of my trip in the great cities of Europe, cities like Athens, Rome, Berlin, and St. Petersburg. 10 I am going to need a lot of money for this trip, I think I am going to need more than six months, too.

✎ Applying Vocabulary: Using Adverbs of Probability

Review what you learned about the adverbs *maybe, perhaps, probably,* and *definitely* on page 175. You may want to use these words when you write a paragraph about something that you are looking forward to.

Study the rules for the placement of these adverbs in sentences about the future.

RULES	EXAMPLES
1. Put *maybe* or *perhaps* before the subject.	My car is old, so maybe I will get a new one. Perhaps she is going to transfer.
2. Put *probably* or *definitely* after *will* or *am/is/are.*	There **will** probably be 15 of us at dinner. We **are** definitely not going to go.

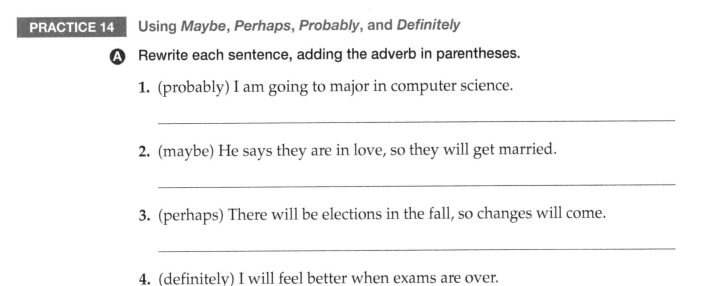

Using *Maybe*, *Perhaps*, *Probably*, and *Definitely*

Ⓐ Rewrite each sentence, adding the adverb in parentheses.

1. (probably) I am going to major in computer science.

   _____

2. (maybe) He says they are in love, so they will get married.

   _____

3. (perhaps) There will be elections in the fall, so changes will come.

   _____

4. (definitely) I will feel better when exams are over.

   _____

Ⓑ Take a sheet of paper. Write four predictions about your future. Use *maybe*, *perhaps*, *probably*, or *definitely* in each sentence.

WRITING ASSIGNMENT

You are going to write a paragraph about something that you are planning and looking forward to in your future. You can write about plans for the near future or the distant future.

📄 Prewrite **STEP 1: Prewrite to get ideas.**

a. Get ready to write by freewriting about your plans for at least five minutes. (See page 134 for an explanation of freewriting and an example.)

b. Find a partner and take turns talking about your plans. Add information to your notes as needed. Tell your partner what you find most interesting about his or her plans.

c. Plan how you will organize the information in your paragraph. You can use time order or listing order. The models on pages 173 and 174 show both ways to organize a paragraph about the future.

STEP 2: Write the first draft.

Use your notes to write a first draft. Your paragraph must begin with a topic sentence. See the writing models on pages 173 and 174 for examples. Your supporting sentences should all relate to your main idea. End your paragraph with a concluding sentence. It should connect to the ideas in your topic sentence. Remember to use *be going to*, not *will*, when you write about plans you have made for the future.

 Edit

STEP 3: Revise and edit the draft.

a. Read your paragraph again. It may help you to read it out loud. Make changes if needed.

b. Do peer review. Sit with a partner and exchange papers. Give each other feedback. Follow the steps on the Peer Review Worksheet.

PEER REVIEW WORKSHEET

Your partner's name: _____

Content

1. Read all of your partner's paragraph.

2. Underline any part of the paragraph you do not understand. Ask your partner to explain it.

3. Circle the topic sentence. If there is no topic sentence, write *TS?* on the paper.

4. Reread the supporting sentences. Ask questions if you want more information, or if it is not clear when events are going to happen.

5. Circle the concluding sentence. If there is no concluding sentence, write *CS?* on the paper.

Format and Language

6. Use this list to check your partner's paragraph. Check (✓) each item as you finish.

   ☐ a subject in every sentence   ☐ the use of verbs with *be going to* and *will*
   ☐ a verb for every subject   ☐ the use of time-order or listing-order words

7. Put a question mark (?) if you are not sure about something.

---

c. Return your partner's paper. Can you say something nice about it?

d. Look at your own paper. If you do not agree with the feedback on it, ask another student or your teacher.

e. Mark any changes you want to make.

Write

STEP 4: Write a new draft.

    a. Take a new sheet of paper, and write a new draft.

    b. Edit your new draft carefully. Then hand it in to your teacher.

Writing Tip

Reading in English can help you write better in English. Read whatever interests you. Choose reading materials that do not have too many new words so that you can read them comfortably.

SELF-ASSESSMENT

In this chapter, you learned to:

○ Use listing-order words in a listing-order paragraph

○ Express future time with *be going to* and *will*

○ Use future time expressions

○ Write complex sentences with future time clauses

○ Identify and correct run-on sentences

○ Write, revise, and edit a paragraph about your future plans

Which ones can you do well? Mark them ✓

Which ones do you need to practice more? Mark them ✗

EXPANSION

 TIMED WRITING

    Students need to write quickly to succeed in academic writing. For example, sometimes students need to do a writing assignment in class or on a test, and they have only a short time to do it.

    To practice writing quickly, you are going to write a paragraph in class. You will have 20 minutes. To complete the assignment in time, follow these steps.

1. Read the writing prompt on page 192 (or the prompt that your teacher gives you). Make sure that you understand the prompt. If you have questions, ask your teacher. (2 minutes)

2. Brainstorm to get ideas. On a sheet of paper, make some notes. Then think about organizing your ideas. Mark up your notes with circles, arrows, and numbers to show the order of information in your paragraph. Write a topic sentence for your paragraph. (6 minutes)

(continued on next page)

3. Write your paragraph. Be sure to include a topic sentence and supporting sentences. (10 minutes)

4. Check your paragraph. Correct any mistakes. (2 minutes)

5. Give your paper to your teacher.

   Prompt: Write a paragraph about an event that is going to happen in your future and how your life will, or will not, be different after it happens.

 YOUR JOURNAL

Continue making entries in your journal. If you cannot think of a topic for a journal entry, try one of these ideas:

- Choose any place in the world and write a weather forecast for this place. Use your imagination, or get current weather information from TV or the Internet.

- Write about the future plans of a friend or family member. How will this person's plans affect you?

- Write about how you will be learning English in the next few weeks or months. What are you going to continue to do? What changes are you going to make?

For more ideas for journal entries, see Appendix A on page 193.

APPENDICES

At the end of each chapter, there are several topic suggestions for writing in your journal. Here are some more ideas for journal writing.

1. Write about your experiences in this class or at the school. Do you have any questions for your teacher?

2. Describe your family. Give your family members' names and tell something about each of them.

3. Do you like music? What kind of music do you listen to? When and where do you listen to music?

4. Write about someone you know at school. What is this person's name? Where is he or she from? What do you know about this person?

5. How is the weather today? Do you like this kind of weather? Name a place with great weather or terrible weather. What is the weather like there?

6. Do you have a best friend? Write about a friend who is important to you. What do you like to do together?

7. Name a place that you think is beautiful. What makes it beautiful?

8. Do you like to watch movies? What kinds of movies do you like most? Name a movie that you have seen recently. Do you think your teacher would like it? Why or why not?

9. Name an island you want to visit. What do you know about this island? Why do you want to go there?

10. What are the seasons of the year where you live? Which season do you like most? Why?

11. Do you watch TV? If you do, tell when, where, and what you watch. If you do not watch TV, tell why not.

12. What do you do for exercise? Do you exercise every day, sometimes, or never?

13. Describe a nice place to visit in your country. It could be a famous place, such as a city or national park, or a place that few people know about.

14. Write about someone you know who has a job. What does this person do? Do you think that he or she has a good job? Tell why or why not.

15. Go to a public place and do some people-watching. Choose a person, and describe him or her. What does the person look like? How old is he or she? What is the person doing? What is he or she wearing?

16. Do you have a pet? Write about your pet, or write about an animal that makes a good pet.

17. Think of someone who was important to you when you were growing up. Who was this person? Why was he or she important in your life?

18. How was this past weekend? Did you have fun? Did you do anything special, or was it just a typical weekend? Describe what you did.

19. Write about a time when you had some good or bad luck.

20. Write about a funny or scary experience you had.

1. The Parts of Speech

The different kinds of words are called **the parts of speech**.

TERM	DEFINITION / FUNCTION	EXAMPLES
Adjective	a word that describes a noun or a subject pronoun	I have a **new** neighbor named Eva. Eva has a **nice** smile. She is **friendly**.
Adverb	a word that usually describes a verb, an adjective, or another adverb, often to tell how, when, or where	The actors talked **fast**. It was **really** difficult to understand. I listened **very** carefully. Meet me **here** at 7:00.
Article	the word *a*, *an*, or *the*, used to introduce a noun	There is **a** café on Green Street. **The** café is called Java's. It is **an** interesting place.
Coordinating conjunction	the word *and*, *but*, *so*, *or*, *nor*, *for*, or *yet*, used to connect two words, phrases, or clauses	Let's have cake **and** ice cream. It is my birthday, **so** I want to celebrate.
Noun	a word for a person, place, thing, or idea	I have a **roommate** at **school**. His **name** is **Mark**. He is from **Hong Kong**. We like the same **music**.
Preposition	a word that is put in front of a noun or pronoun, often to express time, location, or direction	I'll meet you **at** 6:30. Let's meet **in front of** the library. We can walk **to** the movie theater.
Pronoun	a word that takes the place of a noun	Do you know Marta? **She** is a good friend of **mine**. I like **her** very much.
Verb	a word for an action, feeling, or state	Davina **plays** the guitar and sings. She **is** in a band. She **loves** rock music.

2. Additional Grammar Terms

TERM	DEFINITION / FUNCTION	EXAMPLES
Auxiliary verb (*Helping verb*)	a form of *be*, *do*, *have*, or another verb used with a main verb	They **are** fixing my car. I **did** not see the movie. **Can** you swim?
Base form of the verb	the form of a verb without any ending or other change	He likes coffee; I **like** tea. Al went, but we did not **go**. It is going to **be** sunny.
Clause	a group of related words that has a subject and a verb	This is my book. . . . because it was late. After I got up, . . .
Dependent clause	a clause that cannot stand alone as a complete sentence (because of its first word)	. . . because it was late. After I got up, ... when it rains.
Gerund	a verb ending in -*ing* that is used as a noun	**Dancing** is fun. I am sad about **leaving**.
Independent clause	a clause that can stand alone as a complete sentence	The baby slept. **The baby slept** while we drove home.
Main verb	the verb with the most important meaning in a verb phrase	He is going to **call** her. They are **fixing** my car. I did not **see** the movie.
Object	a noun, pronoun, or gerund that receives the action of a verb or follows a preposition	I called **Jim**. I gave **him** the **message**. We were happy about **winning**.
Phrasal verb	a combination of a verb and a particle with its own meaning	It is time to **get up.** He **turned down** the invitation.
Phrase	a group of related words without a subject and verb	I had **a very frightening experience.** It happened **a few days ago.**
Prepositional phrase	a preposition plus a noun, pronoun, or gerund object	The train left **at noon**. Hundreds of people were **on it.**
Subject	a noun or subject pronoun that tells who or what a sentence is about	The **museum** is closed on Mondays. On other days, **it** opens at 9:00 A.M.
Time clause	a clause that tells when the action of an independent clause happens	**Before you go,** please hand in your homework. He found a job **after he graduated.**

1. **Subject Pronouns; Object Pronouns; Possessive Adjectives; Possessive Pronouns**

SUBJECT PRONOUNS			
Singular	**Plural**		
I	we	**I** am a student.	**We** are students.
you	you	**You** are my partner.	**You** are my classmates.
he		**He** is from Japan.	
she	they	**She** is from China.	**They** are from Mexico.
it		**It** is a chair.	

OBJECT PRONOUNS			
Singular	**Plural**		
me	us	Call **me**.	Come with **us**.
you	you	This chair is for **you**.	These chairs are for **you**.
him		I know **him**.	
her	them	I know **her**.	I know **them**.
it		I know **it**.	

POSSESSIVE ADJECTIVES			
Singular	**Plural**		
my	our	This is **my** name.	These are **our** names.
your	your	What is **your** name?	What are **your** names?
his		What is **his** name?	
her	their	What is **her** name?	What are **their** names?
its		What is **its** name?	

POSSESSIVE PRONOUNS			
Singular	**Plural**		
mine	ours	This book is **mine**.	This classroom is **ours**.
yours	yours	That book is **yours**.	That classroom is **yours**.
his		That paper is **his**.	
hers	theirs	That paper is **hers**.	That classroom is **theirs**.

2. Count and Noncount Nouns; Possessive Nouns

Count Nouns

Count nouns can be singular or plural.

SPELLING RULES FOR PLURAL COUNT NOUNS	EXAMPLES	
1. For most count nouns, add -s.	sister / sisters	house / houses
2. For count nouns ending in x, ch, sh, or ss, add -es.	box / boxes	match / matches
3. For most count nouns ending in a consonant + o, add -es.	tomato / tomatoes (Exceptions: photos, pianos)	volcano / volcanoes
4. For count nouns ending in a vowel + y, add -s.	boy / boys	key / keys
5. For count nouns ending in a consonant + y, change the y to i and add -es.	baby / babies	party / parties
6. For most count nouns ending in f or fe, drop the f(e) and add -ves.	loaf / loaves	wife / wives

IRREGULAR COUNT NOUNS	EXAMPLES	
1. Some count nouns have an irregular plural form.	person / **people** man / **men** tooth / **teeth**	child / **children** woman / **women** foot / **feet**
2. Some count nouns have the same form in the singular and the plural.	fish / **fish**	sheep / **sheep**
3. Some count nouns have only a plural form.	— / **jeans** — / **clothes**	— / **pants** — / **(eye)glasses**

Noncount Nouns

Noncount nouns have only one form. These nouns cannot be counted. For example, it is not correct to say *one homework* or *many homeworks*.

COMMON NONCOUNT NOUNS							
Food		**Liquids**		**Substances with Very Small Parts**		**Gases**	
bread	fruit	coffee	oil	dirt	rice	air	nitrogen
butter	lettuce	gasoline	soda	dust	salt	helium	oxygen
cheese	meat	juice	tea	flour	sand	hydrogen	
fish	soup	milk	water	pepper	sugar		

Weather	**Abstract Ideas**		**Problems**	**Other**	
fog	advice	hope	crime	email	money
ice	education	love	noise	furniture	music
rain	happiness	luck	pollution	homework	paper
snow	help	time	traffic	information	work

Some nouns (often nouns for food or drink) can be count or noncount:

COUNT: We would like two **coffees**, please.

NONCOUNT: He drinks a lot of **coffee**.

Possessive Nouns

A **possessive noun** shows the owner of something.

That is **Hiro's** car. = Hiro is the owner of that car. It is his car.

SPELLING RULES FOR POSSESSIVE NOUNS	EXAMPLES
1. Add an apostrophe + s ('s) to singular nouns.	He is my **sister's** son. I am riding **Carlos's** bike.
2. Add an apostrophe + s ('s) to plural nouns that do not end in -s.	Where is the **men's** department? Tell me the **people's** names.
3. Add an apostrophe alone (') to plural nouns that end in -s.	Our **teachers'** offices are on the first floor. The **Smiths'** house is on Maple Street.

3. The Verb *Be*—Present and Past

The Present of *Be*

Statements: Full Forms

AFFIRMATIVE STATEMENTS		
Subject	***Be***	
I	**am**	ready.
We		
You	**are**	in class.
They		
He		
She	**is**	warm.
It		

NEGATIVE STATEMENTS			
Subject	***Be***	***Not***	
I	**am**		late.
We			
You	**are**		at home.
They		**not**	
He			
She	**is**		cold.
It			

Statements: Contractions

AFFIRMATIVE	NEGATIVE	
I'm	**I'm** not	—
we're	**we're** not	we **aren't**
you're	**you're** not	you **aren't**
they're	**they're** not	they **aren't**
he's	**he's** not	he **isn't**
she's	**she's** not	she **isn't**
it's	**it's** not	it **isn't**

Questions and Answers

YES / NO QUESTIONS		
Be	**Subject**	
Am	I	late?
Are	we	
	you	on time?
	they	
Is	he	
	she	ready?
	it	

SHORT ANSWERS							
Yes	**Subject**	**Be**	**No**	**Subject**	**Be**	**Not**	
Yes,	I	am.	No,	I	am		
	we			we			
	you	are.		you	are		
	they			they		not.	
	he			he			
	she	is.		she	is		
	it			it			

INFORMATION QUESTIONS		
Wh- Question Word	**Be**	
Where	**are**	we?
Who	**is**	she?
What	**is**	that?

ANSWERS
We are on Price Street.
She is my sister.
It is a letter for you.

The Past of *Be*

Statements

AFFIRMATIVE STATEMENTS		
Subject	**Be**	
I	**was**	ready.
We		
You	**were**	in class.
They		
He		
She	**was**	warm.
It		

NEGATIVE STATEMENTS			
Subject	**Be**	**Not**	
I	**was**		late.
We			
You	**were**		at home.
They		**not**	
He			
She	**was**		cold.
It			

CONTRACTIONS
was + not = **wasn't** were + not = **weren't**

Questions and Answers

YES / NO QUESTIONS		
Be	**Subject**	
Was	I	late?
Were	we	
	you	on time?
	they	
Was	he	
	she	ready?
	it	

SHORT ANSWERS							
Yes	**Subject**	**Be**	**No**	**Subject**	**Be**	**Not**	
Yes,	I	**was.**	No,	I	**was**		
	we	**were.**		we	**were**	**not.**	
	you			you			
	they			they			
	he	**was.**		he	**was**		
	she			she			
	it			it			

INFORMATION QUESTIONS			ANSWERS
Wh- Question Word	**Be**		
Where	**were**	you?	I was at home.
Who	**was**	that man?	A friend of Rima's.
What	**was**	his name?	Tim.

4. The Simple Present

Statements

AFFIRMATIVE STATEMENTS	
Subject	**Simple Present Verb**
I	
We	
You	**work.**
They	
He	
She	**works.**
It	

NEGATIVE STATEMENTS			
Subject	**Do/ Does**	**Not**	**Base Form of the Main Verb**
I			
We			
You	**do**		
They		**not**	work.
He			
She	**does**		
It			

CONTRACTIONS
do + not = **don't**
does + not = **doesn't**

Questions and Answers

YES / NO QUESTIONS		
Do/Does	**Subject**	**Base Form of the Main Verb**
Do	I	
	we	
	you	
	they	**work?**
Does	he	
	she	
	it	

SHORT ANSWERS							
Yes	**Subject**	**Do/Does**	**No**	**Subject**	**Do/Does**	**Not**	
	I			I			
	we			we			
	you	**do.**		you	**do**		
Yes,	they		No,	they		**not.**	
	he			he			
	she	**does.**		she	**does**		
	it			it			

INFORMATION QUESTIONS ABOUT THE SUBJECT			ANSWERS
Wh- Question Word (subject)	**Simple Present Verb**		
Who	**teaches**	that class?	Ms. Adams.
What	**happens**	on Friday?	We go to the lab.

OTHER INFORMATION QUESTIONS				ANSWERS
Wh- Question Word	**Do / Does**	**Subject**	**Base Form of the Main Verb**	
Where	**do**	you	**work?**	At City Hospital.
Who	**does**	she	**like?**	Paul.
What	**does**	he	**do?**	He is a taxi driver.

Spelling Rules for Third Person Singular Verbs in Affirmative Statements

RULES	EXAMPLES
1. For most verbs, add *-s* to the base form of the verb.	works plays reads writes
2. For verbs ending in *x*, *ch*, *sh*, or *ss*, add *-es*.	boxes kisses watch**es** wash**es**
3. For verbs ending in a consonant + *y*, change the *y* to *i* and add *-es*.	stud**y** / stud**ies** carr**y** / carr**ies** fl**y** / fl**ies**

5. The Present Progressive

Statements

AFFIRMATIVE STATEMENTS			NEGATIVE STATEMENTS			
Subject	***Be***	**Base Form of the Main Verb + *-ing***	**Subject**	***Be***	***Not***	**Base Form of the Main Verb + *-ing***
I	am		I	am		
We			We			
You	are		You	are		
They		working.	They		not	working.
He			He			
She	is		She	is		
It			It			

Contractions: See Appendix C3, page 199, for the contracted forms of *am*, *is*, and *are*.

Questions and Answers

YES / NO QUESTIONS		
Be	**Subject**	**Base Form of the Main Verb + *-ing***
Am	I	
	we	
Are	you	
	they	working?
	he	
Is	she	
	it	

SHORT ANSWERS							
Yes	**Subject**	**Be**	**No**	**Subject**	**Be**	**Not**	
	I	am.		I	am		
	we			we			
	you	are.		you	are		
Yes,	they		No,	they		not.	
	he			he			
	she	is.		she	is		
	it			it			

INFORMATION QUESTIONS ABOUT THE SUBJECT			ANSWERS
Wh- Question Word (subject)	**Is**	**Base Form of the Main Verb + *-ing***	
Who	is	singing?	Janice is.
What	is	happening?	We are having a meeting.

OTHER INFORMATION QUESTIONS				ANSWERS
Wh- Question Word	**Be**	**Subject**	**Base Form of the Main Verb + *-ing***	
Where	are	you	going?	To work.
Who	is	she	calling?	Her mother.
What	is	he	doing?	He is fixing the computer.

Spelling Rules for Verbs Ending in *-ing*

Rules	Examples
1. Add *-ing* to the base form of most verbs.	go / go**ing** read / read**ing** fly / fly**ing**
2. When the base form ends in *e*, drop the *e* and add *-ing*.	mak**e** / mak**ing** writ**e** / writ**ing**
3. When the base form ends in *ie*, change the *ie* to *y* and add *-ing*.	d**ie** / d**ying** l**ie** / l**ying**
4. When the last three letters of the base form are consonant + vowel + consonant, double the final consonant and add *-ing*.	for**get** / forge**tting** s**top** / sto**pping**
5. There are two exceptions to Rule 4: • Do not double *w* or *x*. • Do not double the final consonant when the last syllable is not stressed.	snowing fixing *Stressed:* be**gin** / begi**nning** *Not stressed:* listen / listen**ing**

6. The Simple Past

Regular Verbs in the Simple Past

AFFIRMATIVE STATEMENTS		NEGATIVE STATEMENTS				CONTRACTIONS
Subject	Simple Past Verb	Subject	*Did*	*Not*	Base Form of the Main Verb	
I		I				did + not = **didn't**
We		We				
You		You				
They	**worked.**	They	**did**	**not**	work.	
He		He				
She		She				
It		It				

Questions and Answers

YES / NO QUESTIONS		
Did	Subject	Base Form
Did	I	
	we	
	you	
	they	work?
	he	
	she	
	it	

SHORT ANSWERS							
Yes	Subject	*Did*	*No*	Subject	*Did*	*Not*
Yes,	I		No,	I		
	we			we		
	you			you		
	they	did.		they	did	not.
	he			he		
	she			she		
	it			it		

INFORMATION QUESTIONS ABOUT THE SUBJECT			ANSWERS
Wh- Question Word (subject)	Simple Past Verb		
Who	worked	yesterday?	I did.
What	happened	on Friday?	We watched a movie in class.

OTHER INFORMATION QUESTIONS				ANSWERS
Wh- Question Word	*Did*	Subject	Base Form of the Main Verb	
Where	did	you	walk?	In the park.
Who	did	she	call?	Her sister.
What	did	he	do?	He washed his car.

Spelling Rules for Verbs Ending in *-ed*

RULES	EXAMPLES
1. Add *-ed* to the base form of most regular verbs.	watch**ed** play**ed** listen**ed**
2. When the base form ends in *e*, then add *-d* only.	danc**ed** hop**ed** believ**ed**
3. When the base form ends in a consonant + *y*, drop the *y* and add *-ied*.	stu**dy** / stud**ied** car**ry** / car**ried**
4. When the base form ends in consonant + vowel + consonant, then double the final consonant and add *-ed*.	p**lan** / plan**ned** s**hop** / shop**ped** pre**fer** / prefer**red**
5. There are two exceptions to Rule 4: • Do not double *w* or *x*. • Do not double the final consonant when the last syllable is not stressed.	snow**ed** mix**ed** relax**ed** *Stressed*: re**fer** / refer**red** *Not stressed*: offer / offer**ed**

Irregular Verbs in the Simple Past

For *be*: See Appendix C3, on page 200.

Affirmative statements: See the Irregular Verb Chart on page 208.

Negative statements: Irregular verbs are the same as regular verbs in negative statements.

Questions: For information questions about the subject, use the irregular verb forms shown in the chart. Irregular verbs are the same as regular verbs in *yes / no* questions and other information questions.

7. Irregular Verb Chart

Base Form	Simple Past	Base Form	Simple Past
be	was / were	keep	kept
become	became	know	knew
begin	began	leave	left
blow	blew	let	let
break	broke	lose	lost
bring	brought	make	made
build	built	pay	paid
buy	bought	put	put
catch	caught	quit	quit
choose	chose	ride	rode
come	came	ring	rang
cost	cost	run	ran
cut	cut	say	said
do	did	see	saw
draw	drew	sell	sold
drink	drank	set	set
drive	drove	shake	shook
eat	ate	shoot	shot
fall	fell	shut	shut
feel	felt	sing	sang
fight	fought	sit	sat
find	found	sleep	slept
fit	fit	speak	spoke
fly	flew	spend	spent
forget	forgot	stand	stood
get	got	steal	stole
give	gave	swim	swam
go	went	take	took
grow	grew	teach	taught
have	had	tell	told
hear	heard	think	thought
hide	hid	throw	threw
hit	hit	understand	understood
hurt	hurt	write	wrote

8. Expressing Future Time with *Be Going To* and *Will*

Be Going To

Statements

AFFIRMATIVE STATEMENTS				NEGATIVE STATEMENTS	CONTRACTIONS
Subject	*Be*	*Going To*	Base Form of the Main Verb		
I	am				
We					
You	are			Add *not* after *am*, *is*, or *are*.	See Appendix C3 for the contracted forms of *am*, *is*, and *are*.
They		going to	eat.		
He					
She	is				
It					

Questions and Answers

YES / NO QUESTIONS				SHORT ANSWERS
Be	Subject	*Going To*	Base Form of the Main Verb	
Am	I			
	we			
Are	you			See Appendix C3 for the short answers for questions with *be* in the present tense.
	they	going to	eat?	
	he			
Is	she			
	it			

INFORMATION QUESTIONS ABOUT THE SUBJECT				ANSWERS
Wh- Question Word (subject)	**Is**	**Going To**	**Base Form of the Main Verb**	
Who	is	going to	help?	John is.
What	is	going to	happen?	We are going to take a vote.

OTHER INFORMATION QUESTIONS					ANSWERS
Wh- Question Word	**Be**	**Subject**	**Going To**	**Base Form of the Main Verb**	
Where	are	you	going to	go?	To the beach.
Who	is	she	going to	invite?	All the neighbors.
What	is	he	going to	do?	He is going to find a new job.

Will

Statements

AFFIRMATIVE STATEMENTS			NEGATIVE STATEMENTS				CONTRACTIONS	
Subject	**Will**	**Base Form**	**Subject**	**Will**	**Not**	**Base Form of the Main Verb**	**Affirmative**	**Negative**
I			I				I'll	
We			We				we'll	
You			You				you'll	
They	will	work.	They	will	not	work.	they'll	will + not = **won't**
He			He				he'll	
She			She				she'll	
It			It				it'll	

Questions and Answers

YES / NO QUESTIONS		
Will	**Subject**	**Base Form of the Main Verb**
Will	I we you they he she it	**work?**

SHORT ANSWERS						
Yes	**Subject**	*Will*	*No*	**Subject**	*Will*	*Not*
Yes,	I we you they he she it	**will.**	No,	I we you they he she it	**will**	**not.**

INFORMATION QUESTIONS ABOUT THE SUBJECT			
Wh- **Question Word (subject)**	*Will*	**Base Form of the Main Verb**	
Who	**will**	**help**	tomorrow?
What	**will**	**happen**	next Monday?

ANSWERS
Mary will.
There will be a meeting.

OTHER INFORMATION QUESTIONS			
Wh- **Question Word**	*Will*	*Subject*	**Base Form of the Main Verb**
Where	**will**	the concert	**be?**
Who	**will**	he	**call?**
What	**will**	they	**do?**

ANSWERS
In the park.
His doctor.
They will sell the car.

9. Order of Adjectives

There can be more than one adjective before a noun, as in

There is a <u>nice</u> <u>new</u> <u>Vietnamese</u> restaurant on Main Street.

Adjectives usually go in this order before a noun:

CATEGORIES OF ADJECTIVES	SIZE	OPINION	PHYSICAL DESCRIPTION			ORIGIN	MATERIAL
			Shape	**Age**	**Color**		
EXAMPLES OF ADJECTIVES	big small	good beautiful expensive	round square	old new	red white light blue	English African Japanese	plastic cotton wooden

They live in a beautiful old apartment building.

He drives a small white Korean car.

Use commas + *and* or *or* when you use a series of three adjectives from the same category.

The orange, white, and green flag of Ivory Coast is similar to the Irish flag.

There are no French, German, or Spanish students in the class.

Never put a comma between the last adjective in a series and the noun.

APPENDIX D   SENTENCE TYPES

There are three basic types of sentences: simple, compound, and complex.

Simple Sentences

A simple sentence has one subject-verb combination. See pages 74, 120, and 135 for examples of simple sentences.

Compound Sentences

A compound sentence has two subject-verb combinations (simple sentence + simple sentence). See page 135 for examples of compound sentences.

A compound sentence needs a comma and a coordinating conjunction to connect the simple sentences. There are seven coordinating conjunctions:

COORDINATING CONJUNCTIONS

and	but	for	nor	or	so	yet

Complex Sentences

A complex sentence has one independent clause and one or more dependent clauses.

- An independent clause can stand alone. It can be a simple sentence.

    We didn't go.

    I will call you.

    He watches the news.

- A dependent clause cannot stand alone because it does not express a complete thought.

    because it was raining

    when I get home

    if he has time

Examples of Complex Sentences

INDEPENDENT CLAUSE + DEPENDENT CLAUSE	DEPENDENT CLAUSE, INDEPENDENT CLAUSE
We didn't go because it was raining.	Because it was raining, we didn't go.
I will call you when I get home.	When I get home, I will call you.
He watches the news if he has time.	If he has time, he watches the news.

A dependent clause has a subordinating conjunction + subject + verb. There are many subordinating conjunctions.

Examples of Subordinating Conjunctions

FOR ADVERB CLAUSES			FOR ADJECTIVE CLAUSES			
Time	**Reason**	**Condition**	**People**	**Things**	**Times**	**Places**
as soon as after before when	because since	if unless	who whom that	that which	when	where

Rules for Capitalization

WHEN TO USE A CAPITAL LETTER	EXAMPLES
1. At the beginning of a sentence	**My** name is Merita. **What** is your name?
2. For the pronoun *I*	Hassan and **I** are partners.
3. For people's names and titles (Do not capitalize a title without a name: *Where does the queen live?*)	My dentist's name is **Dr. Parker.** This is a picture of **Queen Elizabeth.**
4. For: nationalities languages religions ethnic groups	**C**anadian, **S**yrian, **B**razilian **E**nglish, **A**rabic, **P**ortuguese **B**uddhism, **I**slam, **C**hristianity **N**ative **A**merican, **L**atino
5. For place names (such as specific countries, cities, rivers, mountains, and so on)	**M**iami, **F**lorida, is in the **U**nited **S**tates. Where are the **R**ocky **M**ountains?
6. For names of buildings, roads, bridges, and other structures	That building is the **W**estin **H**otel. My bank is on **H**igh **S**treet. We saw the **S**tatue of **L**iberty.
7. For names of months, holidays, special time periods, and the days of the week (Do not capitalize the seasons: *winter, spring, summer, fall/autumn.*)	There are thirty days in **A**pril. Do you celebrate **N**ew **Y**ear's **E**ve? When is **R**amadan? My appointment is on **M**onday.
8. For names of organizations (such as businesses, schools, clubs)	My country belongs to the **U**nited **N**ations. He is the president of **N**ike. She is a student at **H**arvard.
9. For abbreviations	He drives a red **VW.** They are students at **UCLA.**
10. For the titles of movies, TV shows, plays, books, newspapers, and magazines • Capitalize the first word and all nouns, pronouns, verbs, adjectives, and adverbs. • Use *italics* when you write a title on the computer. • Underline a title when you write it by hand.	Have you seen *Gone with the Wind*? Who wrote *A Raisin in the Sun*? I used to watch *Sesame Street*. He reads <u>The Boston Globe</u> every day.
11. For the titles of your paragraphs (See page 82)	**M**y **H**ometown **P**lanning for the **F**uture

Punctuation

PUNCTUATION MARK	RULES	EXAMPLES
period	1. Use at the end of a statement.	My name is Anna.
	2. Use to separate dollars and cents.	$10.00
question mark	Use at the end of a question.	What is your name?
exclamation point	1. Use to show surprise or strong emotion.	What a nice idea!
	2. Use to show a command is strong.	Don't forget!
apostrophe	1. Use in place of a letter in a contraction.	he + is = he's
	2. Use to form a possessive noun.	That is Mr. King's office.
quotation marks	Use before and after the exact words that someone spoke.	He said, "Meet me at 9:00."
comma	1. Use between the date and the year and also after the year in a sentence.	It happened on July 1, 1922. May 2, 2013, was my first day on the job.
	2. Use after an introductory word or phrase at the beginning of a sentence.	Finally, add salt and pepper. On Friday, they met for lunch.
	3. Use to separate three or more items in a series.	I like bananas, apples, oranges, and pears.
	4. Use after the first part of a compound sentence.	He loves good food, but he does not like to cook.
	5. Use after a dependent clause that comes first in a complex sentence.	After the class ended, we went for coffee.
	6. Use in large numbers to separate thousands, millions, billions, and so on.	There are 5,280 feet in a mile. She received $8,000,000.

Group 1

Symbol	Meaning	Example of Error
cap	capitalization error	The class meets on <u>m</u>onday. *(cap)*
sing or pl	singular or plural	She has two <u>book</u>. *(pl)*
sp	spelling mistake	He is a <u>colege</u> student. *(sp)*
^	missing word	He ^ my friend.
———	rewrite as shown	I go with ~~my some~~ friends. *(some of my)*

PRACTICE 1

I would like to introduce myself. <u>my</u> name is Isabel Angara. *(cap)*

I ^ from the Philippines. I ^ married. ~~I and my husband~~ have one son and one <u>daugther</u>. *(My husband and I)* *(sp)*

I take two classes. I want to learn <u>e</u>nglish. I want to study <u>computer</u>. *(cap)* *(pl)*

Group 2

Symbol	Meaning	Example of Error
ww	wrong word	He makes cars in a Honda <u>fabric</u>. ^{ww}
∼	wrong word order	It is a restaurant nice.
✕	delete word	Do you like ~~the~~ hip-hop music?
agr	error in subject-verb agreement	You <u>was</u> absent yesterday. ^{agr}
⌒	connect or close up space	I some times watch the news. He speaks English, Spanish, and French.

PRACTICE 2

Alessandro Santos has a life very busy. He has nineteen years old. ^{ww}

He is a college student, and he works, too. He delivers ~~the~~ pizzas

for Pizza Express. He <u>have</u> classes during the week, and he <u>work</u> on ^{agr} ^{agr}

week ends. He <u>is</u> not have much time free. Sometimes he ~~is~~ plays ^{ww}

basket ball with his friends.

Group 3

Symbol	Meaning	Example of Error
P	punctuation error	She was born on March_P 13, 1987.
vt	wrong verb tense	Last night, I <u>see</u> a good movie. *vt*
wf	wrong word form	We are going <u>shop</u> downtown. *wf*
FRAG	sentence fragment	I went home. Because I was tired. *FRAG*
RO	run-on sentence	He gets up early he takes a shower. *RO*

PRACTICE 3

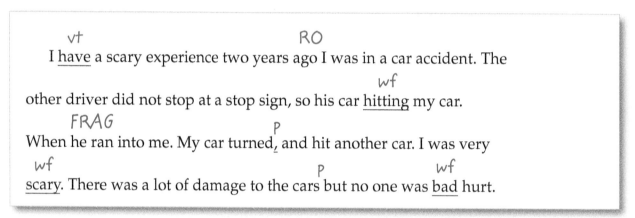

       vt   *RO*

I <u>have</u> a scary experience two years ago I was in a car accident. The
                                          wf

other driver did not stop at a stop sign, so his car <u>hitting</u> my car.
   FRAG   *P*

When he ran into me. My car turned, and hit another car. I was very
wf   *P*   *wf*

<u>scary</u>. There was a lot of damage to the cars but no one was <u>bad</u> hurt.

INDEX

A

A, an, 94
Action verbs, 10, 118
Adjectives
 after *be*, 61
 explanation of, 61, 194
 with nouns, 61, 94
 order of, 212
 plus prepositions, 132, 147
 possessive, 196
 prepositions following, 132, 147
Adverbs
 explanation of, 175, 194
 of frequency, 75–79 117
 of probability, 175, 188
After, 162, 164, 184
Ago, 159
And, 121, 137, 180
Articles
 a, an, 94, 194
 the, 96, 194
At, 79, 99
Auxiliary verbs, 195

B

Base form of the verb, 195
Be
 basic sentence patterns with, 13
 contractions, 199–200
 past tense, 140–141, 200–201
 present tense, 12, 58, 199
 questions, 200, 201
Be going to, 178, 209–210
Before, 162, 164
Brainstorming, 103
But, 137

C

Capitalization, 8, 81–82, 214
Chronological order, 72, 133
Clauses
 dependent, 195, 213
 explanation of, 195, 213
 future time, 183, 184
 independent, 163, 183, 195, 213
 past time, 163–164
Commas, 139, 212, 215
Complex sentences, 163, 183, 213
Compound sentences, 136–137

Concluding sentences, 92, 156
Conjunctions
 coordinating, 136–138, 194
 subordinating, 164, 183, 213
Connectors. *See Conjunctions*
Contractions
 with *be*, 199
 with *did*, 205
 with *do/does*, 201
 with *will*, 210
 Writing Tip about, 150
Controlling ideas, 48
Coordinating conjunctions, 136–138, 194, 212
Correction symbols, 216–218
Count nouns, 197

D

Dates, commas in, 139
Dependent clauses, 195, 213
Directions, words for, 91, 102
Do
 as auxiliary verb, 58, 201–202
 contractions with, 201
Double spacing, 28
Drafts
 first, 16
 illustrations of, 39–40
 Writing Tips about, 19, 42, 105, 169

E

Editing
 explanation of, 17
 Writing Tips about, 42, 105
Evidence, 112

F

Feedback, 38–39
First drafts
 explanation of, 16
 Writing Tip about reviewing, 19
For, 79, 160
Format
 page, 26–29
 paragraph, 5
Fragments, 166, 183

Freewriting
 example, 134
 explanation of, 134
 Writing Tip about, 148
Frequency, adverbs of, 75–77, 117
From, 79
Future
 with *be going to*, 178, 209–210
 plans, 173, 178, 180
 predictions, 178, 180
 time clauses, 183, 184
 time expressions, 182
 with *will*, 180
 Writing Tip about expressing
  plans or predictions, 179

G

Gerunds
 explanation of, 147, 195
 as objects of prepositions, 147
Go + -ing verbs, 47, 63

H

Have
 as action versus non-action verb,
  118
 simple present, 35
Headings, 26–29
Helping verbs. *See Auxiliary verbs.*

I

In, 79, 99, 160, 182
-ing verbs
 as gerunds, 147
 in the present progressive, 114
 spelling rules for, 205
Indenting, 5
Independent clauses, 163, 183, 195
Information questions
 be, 200, 201
 future, 210, 211
 present progressive, 204
 simple past, 206, 207
 simple present, 202
Irregular count nouns, 31, 197
Irregular verbs, past tense, 144,
  206–208

J

Journals
    example of journal entry, 21
    explanation of, 20
    FAQs about, 20
    suggested topics for, 21, 43, 68,
        87, 106, 128, 151, 171, 192, 193
Jobs, words for, 110

L

Last, 159
Lines
    skipping, 26–27
    spacing between, 28
Listing order
    examples of paragraphs with,
        131, 158, 176
    explanation of, 133
    listing-order words, 176
Location, prepositions for, 99

M

Main clauses. *See Independent clauses*
Main verbs, 195
Margins, 26–28
Models
    explanation of, 2
    Writing Models, 2–3, 23–24,
        45–46, 70–71, 89–90, 108–109,
        130–131, 153–154, 173–174

N

Names, words for, 3
Negative verbs, 58, 114, 143–144,
    199, 200–201, 203, 205, 207
Next, 182
Non-action verbs, 10, 118
Noncount nouns, 198
Nouns
    with adjectives, 61, 94
    with articles, 94, 96
    count, 197
    explanation of, 30, 194
    noncount, 198
    plus prepositions, 79
    possessive, 198
    regular versus irregular, 31, 197
    singular versus plural, 31
    spelling rules for plural, 197

O

Objects, 195
Object pronouns, 196
On, 79, 99, 160
Or, 121, 180
Organizing ideas, 72, 133

P

Page format, 26–28
Paragraphs
    body of, 92
    concluding sentences in, 92, 156
    explanation of, 4
    format, 5
    supporting sentences in, 92, 111
    topic sentences in, 48, 92, 111, 156
    unity, 112
Parts of speech
    explanation of, 61, 194
    Writing Tip about, 76
Past tense. *See Simple past*
Past time clauses, 163–164
Past time expressions, 141, 159–161
Peer review
    explanation of, 17, 38–39
    illustration of peer-reviewed first
        draft, 39
    worksheets for, 41, 66, 85, 105,
        126, 149, 169, 190
Periods, 8, 215
Phrasal verbs, 72, 195
Phrases
    explanation of, 195
    prepositional, 79, 100, 160, 195
Plans, expressing future, 173, 178,
    180
Possessives
    adjectives, 196
    nouns, 198
    pronouns, 196
Predictions about the future, 178,
    180
Prepositional phrases
    for describing past time, 160
    explanation of, 79, 195
    placement in sentences, 100
Prepositions
    before and *after* as, 162
    to describe location, 99
    explanation of, 79, 194
    in prepositional phrases, 79, 195
    to show time, 79, 162
    used after adjectives, 132, 147
Present progressive
    functions, 116
    questions and answers, 204

    spelling rules, verbs ending in
        -ing, 205
    statements, 114, 203
    time expressions used with, 117
Present tense. *See Simple present*
Prewriting
    brainstorming, 103
    explanation of, 16
    freewriting, 134
    Writing Tip about, 65
Probability, adverbs of, 175, 188
Process
    explanation of, 16
    steps in the writing process,
        16–17
Pronouns
    explanation of, 194
    object, 196
    possessive, 196
    subject, 33, 196
Punctuation
    apostrophes, 198, 215
    commas, 139, 215
    exclamation points, 215
    periods, 8, 215
    question marks, 8, 215
    quotation marks, 215

R

Regular verbs. *See Simple past*
Relevant versus irrelevant
    sentences, 112
Reviewer's checklists. *See Peer
    review worksheets*
Revising
    explanation of, 17
    Writing Tips about, 105, 169
Run-on sentences, 186

S

Sentence fragments, 166, 183
Sentence patterns, 74, 120–122, 135,
    136–138, 163, 183
Sentences
    complex, 163, 183, 213
    compound, 136–138
    concluding, 92, 156
    explanation of, 5
    fragments, 166, 183
    with future time clauses, 183
    with past time clauses, 163–164
    run-on, 186
    simple, 74, 120–122, 135
    statements versus questions, 6
    subjects of, 5, 55–56, 120–122, 135

supporting, 92, 111
topic, 48
types of, 74, 120–122, 135, 136–137, 163, 183, 212–213
verbs in, 5, 56, 120–122, 135
Writing Tip about sentence variety, 122
Simple form of the verb. *See Base form of the verb.*
Simple past
  be, 140–141
  function of, 140
  irregular verbs, 144, 206–207
  questions and answers, 206–207
  spelling rules, verbs ending in *-ed*, 207
  statements, 140–146, 205, 207
Simple present
  be, 12, 199–200
  function of, 35, 117
  questions and answers, 202
  spelling rules, third person singular, 35, 203
  statements, 35, 58, 201
Simple sentences, 74, 120–122, 135
Skipping lines, 26, 27
So, 137
Spacing
  between lines, 26–28
  between words, 28
Spelling rules
  plural count nouns, 197
  simple present verbs, third person singular, 35, 203
  verbs ending in *-ed*, 207
  verbs ending in *-ing*, 205
Stative verbs, 118
Steps in the writing process, 16–17
Subject pronouns, 33, 196
Subjects of sentences
  explanation of, 5, 55, 74, 195
  subject-verb combinations, 74
Subordinating conjunctions, 164, 213
Supporting sentences, 92, 111

T

Tenses. *See Future, Present progressive, Simple past, Simple present*
The, 96
Their versus *there*, 97
There is/are
  statements, 97
  versus *they are* and *their*, 97
This, 182

Time clauses
  explanation of, 195
  future, 183, 184
  past, 163, 164
Time expressions
  explanation of, 79
  future, 182
  past, 141, 159–160
  prepositional phrases as, 79
Time order, 72, 133
Time-order words, 72
Titles
  and page format, 26, 28
  rules for capitalizing, 82, 214
  Writing Tip about, 52
To, 79
Topics
  of paragraphs, 4
  suggested for journals, 21, 43, 68, 87, 106, 128, 151, 171, 192, 193
  of topic sentences, 48
  Writing Tip about choosing a topic, 124
Topic sentences
  controlling idea in, 48
  explanation of, 48
  links to concluding sentences, 156
  support for, 92, 111
  titles and, 52
  topic in, 48
  Writing Tips about, 52, 104

U

Unity, 112

V

Verbs. *See also* Be, *Future, Present progressive, Sentences, Simple past, Simple present*
  action, 10, 119
  in complete sentences, 56
  explanation of, 10, 194
  have, 119
  irregular, 144
  non-action, 10, 118
  regular, 142–144

W

Wh- questions. *See Information questions*
When, 164
Will, 180, 210–211
Word families, 155
Word partners, 25, 37

Words at the end of a line, 26
Words for directions, 91, 102
Words for jobs, 110
Writing process
  illustrated, 17
  steps in, 16
Writing Tips
  about choosing a topic, 124
  about considering readers' needs, 168
  about contractions, 150
  about editing, 42, 105
  about freewriting, 148
  about the parts of speech, 76
  about prewriting, 65
  about reading to become a better writer, 191
  about reviewing a first draft, 19
  about revising, 105, 169
  about sentence variety, 122
  about titles, 52
  about topic sentences, 52, 104
  about using *I (do not) think*, 179

Y

Yes/no questions and short answers
  be, 200, 201
  future, 209, 211
  present progressive, 204
  simple past, 206, 207
  simple present, 202

CREDITS

Photo credits:

Page xiii: ESB Professional/Shutterstock; **xiv:** Everett Historical/Shutterstock; **xv (left):** Image Source/Glow Images; **1** ESB Professional/Shutterstock; **8** Blend Images/Shutterstock; **14:** Take A Pix Media/Shutterstock; **22 (top):** AsiaPix/Asia Images Group Pte Ltd/Alamy Stock Photo; **22 (bottom):** Image Source/Glow Images; **30:** Image Source/Glow Images; **37:** Wavebreakmedia/Shutterstock; **44:** Ollyy/Shutterstock; **45:** Corbis Premium RF/Alamy Stock Photo; **47:** CandyBox Images/Shutterstock; **49 (top):** CREATISTA/Shutterstock; **49 (bottom):** Wendy Kaveney Photograph/Shuttertsock; **50:** Nancy Bauer/Shutterstock; **51:** MediaPunch/ Shutterstock; **57:** Piyawat Nandeenopparit/Shutterstock; **59** Roka Pics/ Shutterstock; **64 (A):** Alohaflaminggo/Shutterstock; **64 (B):** ESB Professional/ Shutterstock, **64 (C):** JGI/Jamie Grill/Blend/GlowImages, **64 (D):** IS098V2U1/ Cultura Creative (RF)/Alamy Stock Photo; **69:** Dex Image/Alamy Stock Photo; **73:** Stephanie Frey/Shutterstock; **74:** Radius Images/Alamy Stock Photo; **76:** PhotoSGH/Shutterstock; **78:** Wasu Watcharadachaphong/ Shutterstock; **80:** Andrey Armyagov/Shutterstock; **83:** Everett Historical/ Shutterstock; **88:** Newphotoservice/Shutterstock; **90:** Corepics VOF/ Shutterstock; **93:** Daniel Fung/Shutterstock; **94:** Evgenymate/Shutterstock; **95:** Doug Lemke/Shutterstock; **107 (top):** AVAVA/Shutterstock; **107 (bottom):** Solis Images/Shutterstock; **108:** Oleksiy Maksymenko Photography/Alamy Stock Photo; **109:** SDI Productions/E+/Getty Images; **112:** Hill Street Studios/ Tetra Images/Alamy Stock Photo; **113:** Volodymyr Goinyk/Shutterstock; **121 (left):** Evgeny Kostishin/Shutterstock; **121 (right):** Impact Photography/ Shutterstock; **123** Phovoir/Shutterstock; **125 (1):** Maximult/Shutterstock; **125 (2):** Rob Marmion/Shutterstock; **125 (3):** Phovoir/Shutterstock; **125 (4):** Jim Arbogast/Photodisc/GettyImages; **129:** Sirtravelalot/Shutterstock; **133:** Fuse/Corbis/Getty Images; **134:** Tetra Images/Alamy Stock Photo; **136:** Joyfull/Shutterstock; **152:** Imagenavi/Getty Images; **157:** Todd Arena/123RF; **158:** Assawin Chomjit/123RF; **159:** Scott Rothstein/Shutterstock; **160:** Nick White/Image Source/Alamy Stock Photo; **161:** D and D Photo Sudbury/Shutterstock; **172:** Mimagephotography/Shutterstock; **177:** Blend Images/SuperStock; **185:** Dasha Petrenko/Shutterstock; **188:** ChameleonsEye/ Shutterstock.

Illustration credits:

Accurate Art: pp. 91, 92; **Steve Attoe:** p. 61; **Mapping Specialists:** pp. 99, 102; **Steve Schulman:** pp. 7, 17, 32, 48, 60, 115, 120, 137; **Albert Tan:** pp. 42, 116, 187; **Chris Vallo:** pp. 10, 34, 146, 166, 184